# The Black Archive #11

# THE EVIL OF
# THE DALEKS

# By Simon Guerrier

Published in 2017 by Obverse Books

Cover Design © Cody Schell

Text © Simon Guerrier, 2017

## Also Available

*The Black Archive #1: Rose* by Jon Arnold
*The Black Archive #2: The Massacre* by James Cooray Smith
*The Black Archive #3: The Ambassadors of Death* by LM Myles
*The Black Archive #4: Dark Water / Death in Heaven* by Philip
      Purser-Hallard
*The Black Archive #5: Image of the Fendahl* by Simon Bucher-Jones
*The Black Archive #6: Ghost Light* by Jonathan Dennis
*The Black Archive #7: The Mind Robber* by Andrew Hickey
*The Black Archive #8: Black Orchid* by Ian Millsted
*The Black Archive #9: The God Complex* by Paul Driscoll
*The Black Archive #10: Scream of the Shalka* by Jon Arnold

## Coming Soon

*The Black Archive #12: Pyramids of Mars* by Kate Orman
*The Black Archive #13: Human Nature / The Family of Blood* by
      Naomi Jacobs and Philip Purser-Hallard
*The Black Archive #14: The Ultimate Foe* by James Cooray Smith
*The Black Archive #15: Carnival of Monsters* by Ian Potter
*The Black Archive #16: The Twin Dilemma* by Gordon Ridout
*The Black Archive #17: Full Circle* by John Toon
*The Black Archive #18: Marco Polo* by Dene October
*The Black Archive #19: The Impossible Planet / The Satan Pit* by
      Simon Bucher-Jones
*The Black Archive #20: Face the Raven* by Sarah Groenewegen
*The Black Archive #21: Heaven Sent* by Kara Dennison
*The Black Archive #22: Hell Bent* by Alyssa Franke
*The Black Archive #23: The Curse of Fenric* by Una McCormack
*The Black Archive #24: The Time Warrior* by Matthew Kilburn
*The Black Archive #25: Doctor Who (1996)* by Paul Driscoll
*The Black Archive #26: The Dæmons* by Matt Barber

For Andrew Pixley

# CONTENTS

# OVERVIEW

**Serial Title:** *The Evil of the Daleks*

**Writer:** David Whitaker

**Director:** Derek Martinus, Timothy Combe[1]

**Original UK Transmission Dates:** 20 May 1967 – 1 July 1967

**Running Time:** 
Episode 1: 24m 07s

Episode 2: 25m 13s

Episode 3: 24m 27s

Episode 4: 24m 43s

Episode 5: 25m 23s

Episode 6: 24m 48s

Episode 7: 24m 33s

**UK Viewing Figures:** Episode 1: 8.1 million

Episode 2: 7.5 million

Episode 3: 6.1 million

Episode 4: 5.3 million

Episode 5: 5.1 million

Episode 6: 6.8 million

Episode 7: 6.1 million

---

[1] Dalek fight film sequence in episode 7 only.

**Regular cast:** Patrick Troughton (Dr Who), Frazer Hines (Jamie), Deborah Watling (Victoria Waterfield)

**Guest Cast:** Alec Ross (Bob Hall), Griffith Davies (Kennedy), John Bailey (Edward Waterfield), Geoffrey Colville (Perry), Robert Jewell, Gerald Taylor, John Scott Martin, Murphy Grumbar, Ken Tyllsen (Daleks), Roy Skelton, Peter Hawkins (Dalek voices), Jo Rowbottom (Mollie Dawson), Marius Goring (Theodore Maxtible), Brigit Forsyth (Ruth Maxtible), Windsor Davies (Toby), Gary Watson (Arthur Terrell), Sonny Caldinez (Kemel)

**Antagonists:** The Emperor Dalek, Maxtible, the Daleks

**Novelisation:** *Doctor Who: The Evil of the Daleks* by John Peel. **The Target Doctor Who Library** #155.

**Sequels and Prequels:** 'Bringer of Darkness' (comic, 1993), *Children of the Revolution* (comic, 2012), 'Father Figure' (short story, 2006).

**Responses:**

'So what is it that makes *The Evil of the Daleks* the most compelling of all the so-called missing stories?'

[Marcus Hearn, 'Alchemy and Apocalypse', *Doctor Who Magazine* #265]

'If only we could see. It's almost a certainty that'll never happen, which is sad. It means I can find no other reason to revisit *The Evil of the Daleks*. Human factor? Dalek factor? To coin a risible phrase, for me it just doesn't have the likeability factor.'

[Graham Kibble-White, 'Missing in Action: *The Evil of the Daleks*', *Doctor Who Magazine* #498]

# SYNOPSIS

## Episode 1

In 1960s London **the Doctor** and **Jamie** search for the TARDIS, which has been unexpectedly taken from Gatwick Airport by lorry. A mechanic, **Bob Hall**, gives them the name of the removal company, but the Doctor realises that he is an impostor and follows him to a meeting with a man named **Kennedy**. Clues left by the two men lead the Doctor and Jamie to the Tricolour coffee bar where they are met by another man, **Perry**. He arranges for them to meet his employer that evening.

Hall, Kennedy and Perry have been working to lure the time-travellers to **Edward Waterfield**, a dealer in Victorian antiques who wears old-fashioned clothes and has trouble with 1960s idioms. His wares are all in mint condition, leading Perry to believe he is selling fakes. Kennedy is also suspicious, and spies on his employer. He breaks into the secret room where Waterfield's deliveries arrive, but while he is busy cracking Waterfield's safe, a **Dalek** materialises and kills him.

## Episode 2

Finding Kennedy dead, Waterfield hastily sets a trap in the secret room. The Doctor and Jamie arrive cautiously early for their appointment at the antiques shop, and meet an equally furtive Perry. They find the body, and Perry goes to fetch help. Jamie triggers Waterfield's trap, releasing gas that renders the Doctor and Jamie unconscious. Waterfield finds them and activates a mechanism. Perry returns with the police to discover that they have vanished.

The Doctor and Jamie wake in 1866, in the house of **Theodore Maxtible**. Along with Waterfield they meet Maxtible, his daughter **Ruth** and their maid **Mollie**. As Jamie has already guessed, Waterfield's antiques are imported directly from the Victorian era. However, the business was just a front for Waterfield's real aim of fetching the Doctor and Jamie into the past. Waterfield and Maxtible's experiments with time-travel, using mirrors and static electricity in a 'time cabinet', attracted the attention of the Daleks, who have taken over the house and are holding Waterfield's daughter **Victoria** hostage. The Daleks need the Doctor to carry out tests on Jamie, to help them isolate the 'human factor' that has allowed humanity repeatedly to defeat them. They have the TARDIS, which they threaten to destroy if the Doctor and Jamie do not cooperate. However, Jamie has been abducted by **Toby**, a thug with a cosh.

## Episode 3

Toby is in the pay of Ruth's eccentric and unstable fiancé **Arthur Terrall**. He asks Jamie urgently where Victoria is, only to then insist calmly that he knows she is safe in Paris. The Doctor finds Jamie and takes him back to the house.

The Doctor is to observe and record Jamie's reactions during a staged rescue of Victoria from captivity in the south wing of the house. He must analyse these outputs to identify the 'human factor', and introduce it into three Daleks who have been brought from their planet, Skaro, in a dormant state. Jamie is angry with the Doctor for cooperating with Maxtible, but the Doctor explains that Waterfield's daughter is being held prisoner and that Jamie must not attempt to rescue her. Jamie naturally sets out to do so.

After trying to blackmail Terrall, Toby steals his house-keys and breaks into Maxtible's laboratory, where a Dalek murders him. Jamie negotiates a booby-trap at the doorway to the south wing, but is confronted inside by a mute Turkish wrestler, **Kemel**, whom Maxtible has told to stand guard.

## Episode 4

During the ensuing fight, Kemel falls out of a window and Jamie has to rescue him. As Jamie continues his search, Kemel saves him from a trap, and they join forces. They avoid another trap thanks to a sudden hunch of Jamie's, and establish that Victoria is being held in a room off the minstrels' gallery of the banqueting hall. Jamie rejects Kemel's suicidal attempt at a rescue plan. In the Daleks' observation room, the Doctor concludes that the human factor must include mercy, instinct and self-preservation.

In despair after finding Toby's body, Waterfield tells Maxtible that he will confess to the authorities as soon as Victoria is safe. Terrall intervenes to prevent Maxtible from shooting Waterfield in the back. Maxtible confronts a Dalek instead, reminding it that he has been promised the knowledge of how to transmute base metal into gold. Ruth fears that Terrall has fallen under her father's influence, and begs him to leave with her.

Jamie and Kemel incapacitate a Dalek guard by catapulting it into a burning fireplace, then climb up to the gallery, straight into a Dalek ambush.

## Episode 5

Jamie and Kemel destroy one Dalek by hurling it to the floor of the banqueting hall, then barricade themselves into the lumber room where Victoria has been kept. Victoria cannot remember how she first fell into the Daleks' hands: in fact she was mesmerised by Maxtible, who now compels Mollie to forget her suspicion that Victoria is being kept in the house. Terrall, too, is under some form of external compulsion, though of a technological kind. He extracts Victoria from the box-room through a secret passage, but Victoria escapes and runs away. While Kemel follows Victoria, Jamie finds Terrall and a swordfight ensues. The Doctor releases Terrall from the Daleks' control, urging him to leave at once with Ruth. Meanwhile Kemel finds Victoria in the laboratory, where a Dalek forces him to carry her into Maxtible's time cabinet.

The Doctor's observations are complete and he has isolated 'the better part' of humanity: 'courage, pity, chivalry, friendship, even compassion'. Over Waterfield's objections he has installed these in the dormant Daleks, theoretically creating a Dalek super-race capable of overcoming humanity. Jamie also condemns him roundly, but the augmented Daleks prove to be friendly and begin playing a game.

## Episode 6

The Doctor expects the childish Daleks – who he names **Alpha**, **Beta** and **Omega** – to mature within hours. They accept the Doctor and Jamie as 'friends', but follow a general summons to return to Skaro. Waterfield realises that Maxtible gave Victoria to the Daleks for personal gain, and the two men argue. Discovering that the Daleks have planted a bomb in the house, Maxtible flees through the time cabinet to Skaro, followed by the remaining Daleks, then by Jamie, the Doctor and Waterfield. The house explodes.

The Doctor's party arrive outside the Dalek city where Victoria, Kemel and Maxtible are being held, and make their way in. They meet a Dalek falsely claiming to be Omega, but the Doctor sees through the trick and pushes the Dalek into a chasm. They follow a sound of screaming (voluntary on Maxtible's part, less so on Victoria's) to the city's control centre and meet the vast, immobile **Emperor Dalek**.

Defiantly, the Doctor tells the Emperor his three altered Daleks will start a rebellion on Skaro, but the Emperor reveals the true purpose of their work. Isolating the human factor has enabled the Daleks to identify the contrasting 'Dalek factor': 'to obey, to fight, to destroy, to exterminate'. The Emperor now has the TARDIS, and orders the Doctor to spread the Dalek factor through time, converting humans into Daleks throughout Earth's history.

## Episode 7

In the city's detention chamber, Maxtible is deceived by the promise of his alchemical secret into passing through an archway, which instils him with the Dalek factor. He apparently mesmerises the Doctor into following him, but the Doctor, who is unaffected by the process because he is not from Earth, only pretends to be similarly converted. After Omega questions an order, the Emperor Dalek commands that all Daleks must pass through the archway, but the Doctor has surreptitiously switched the Dalek and human factors, and soon these Daleks are playing like children. When a superior confronts them, they disobey orders. Soon a full-scale Dalek rebellion is under way, which the Doctor directs towards the Emperor's control centre. Jamie, Kemel and Victoria flee the city to find the TARDIS, but meet Maxtible. He kills Kemel before obeying a summons to defend the control centre. Meanwhile Waterfield has stayed to help the Doctor, and is caught in Dalek crossfire. Maxtible arrives in time to see the Emperor destroyed, and the city follows shortly afterwards.

The Doctor finds Jamie and Victoria, who will join them in the TARDIS. He speculates that they have seen the 'end of the Daleks forever'.

# INTRODUCTION

'Oh, we know it's gone. That's the whole point.'

[Jamie][2]

The **Doctor Who** story *The Evil of the Daleks* was first broadcast on BBC One in the UK over seven weeks from 20 May to 1 July 1967. It was repeated once in the UK in 1968, and then the original two-inch videotapes of all seven episodes were wiped.

Today, that seems extraordinary – horrific – because we expect television to endure. If we miss the first broadcast of an episode, there's no reason to think we'll **never** see it. Things used to be very different.

As Richard Molesworth explains in *Wiped! Doctor Who's Missing Episodes* (2013), the expensive two-inch videotapes used to record **Doctor Who** and other programmes were routinely wiped and reused[3]. It was also argued that repeating old programmes meant doing those working in TV out of money, as fees for repeats were usually less than for newly commissioned work. In fact, *The Evil of the Daleks* was the only **Doctor Who** story to be repeated in its entirety in the 1960s. Until the 1980s, there was also little facility for – or perceived interest in – making old programmes available to the public to buy. Television was largely seen by those making and those watching it as being like theatre: a live event (even if the

---

[2] *The Evil of the Daleks* episode 1.
[3] Molesworth, Richard, *Wiped! Doctor Who's Missing Episodes*, p43.

programme had been pre-recorded, not broadcast live). Once the performance was over, it was gone.

Copies of *The Evil of the Daleks* made on 16mm film were transmitted in Australia, Hong Kong, Singapore and New Zealand in 1969 and 1970. The last ever transmission of the story in its entirety was on NZBC in the Dunedin area of New Zealand[4], between 4 September and 16 October 1970[5]. All 16mm versions of the story seem to have been destroyed during the 1970s except for one print of episode 2, a copy of which is now held in the BBC archive and has been released on VHS and DVD.

It's possible that the story still existed in its entirety on 16mm film at the BBC as late as autumn 1976, and that the last person to see it in full was **Doctor Who**'s former script editor, Terrance Dicks. At the time, Dicks was researching a documentary about **Doctor Who** and viewed a number of old stories held in the BBC archive. His 'Summary of recommended available material' includes *The Evil of the Daleks*, with the description 'The Doctor encounters the Daleks again, this time in Victorian London.' As the Victorian part of the story **isn't** set in London, he wasn't watching especially closely. However, Dicks cannot now recall if what he saw was just episode 2 or the entire story[6].

---

[4] In New Zealand, 'Television was broadcast on a regional basis – with transmitters in Auckland, Wellington, Christchurch and Dunedin – until 29 October 1973, when television across the country became fully networked' ('New Zealand', *BroaDWcast* ).

[5] Molesworth, *Wiped!*, pp462-3.

[6] Molesworth, *Wiped!*, p201. By late 1978 the archive held no episodes from *The Evil of the Daleks* and episode 2 was returned in

Whatever the case, it seems no one has watched *The Evil of the Daleks* in its entirety for more than 40 years. It was gone before the author of this book was born. Even those old enough to have seen it did so just once, perhaps twice, all that time ago. But how can we analyse a text that no longer exists?

This is not a unique situation. James Cooray Smith's *The Black Archive #2: The Massacre* (2016) is devoted to a **Doctor Who** story from which **no** episodes survive. But historians of the theatre also attempt to reconstruct and understand plays that were never recorded. There are inherent problems in this:

> 'Written descriptions of acting performances seldom succeed in arousing the reader; when their moment has gone, they fade into the mist of old, jumbled letters and photographs; faces look beyond us from the past as distant as tomorrow.'[7]

These are the words of Marius Goring, the actor who portrays Maxtible in *The Evil of the Daleks*, introducing a book that attempts to reconstruct the play *The Bells* (1871) by Leopold Lewis as performed by the great Victorian actor Henry Irving. The book reproduces Irving's own typescript of the play with photographs, illustrations, floor plans, the original score, contemporary reviews and an eye-witness account of one particular performance. Editor

---

May 1987, having been found in a car boot sale in 1983. Intriguingly, we don't know how it got there, or whether it is the same copy of the episode Dicks viewed in 1976. See *Wiped!* for a full account.

[7] Goring, Marius, 'Foreword'. Mayer, David, ed, *Henry Irving and the Bells*, pxi.

David Mayer, reader in drama at the University of Manchester, clearly researched widely to provide notes that offer insight and context.

While there are no known recordings of Irving in *The Bells*, we do better with *The Evil of the Daleks* where there is a surviving episode and a variety of sources in different media. Taken together, these sources give a good overall impression of what we are missing – but the sources are only available separately, and some are easier to come by than others, as we'll see.

New research can offer additional insights – such as the direct influence of *The Bells* and Henry Irving on *The Evil of the Daleks*, as we'll see in Chapter 2. Yet there are still so many gaps. This book hopes to better understand what *The Evil of the Daleks* is and what it means, but cannot be a definitive account. We can get so close, but until the missing six episodes are returned to the BBC – if they ever are – the story will remain tantalisingly out of reach. Perhaps that's part of the appeal. Richard Molesworth argues that, 'put simply, the missing episodes have made **Doctor Who** much, much more interesting.'[8]

Or, as Goring exclaimed of *The Bells*, 'If only we knew more!'[9]

---

[8] Molesworth, *Wiped!*, p423.
[9] Goring, 'Foreword', pxi.

# CHAPTER 1: LONDON, 20 JULY 1966

JAMIE

Doctor, you know you told me outside it said 'Genuine Victorian antiques'? Well, all the stuff in here's brand new.

DOCTOR

Hmm, you've noticed that... Except that all these things are not reproductions. They're all genuine.[10]

## The First Six Minutes

This book offers a critical analysis of *The Evil of the Daleks*, but with six of the seven episodes missing from the archive, we can only analyse a version of the story reconstructed from partial sources. We'll discuss how the different sources affect our response in Chapter 4, but to begin with let's briefly use them to reconstruct the opening minutes of episode 1. Having established what the text is, we can then address what it means.

In common with all **Doctor Who** episodes of the period, there is no pre-titles sequence at the beginning of episode 1 of *The Evil of the Daleks*. We start with the opening titles, which were of 22s duration according to the running order included with the camera script – the version used in the studio recording of the episode, detailing how the cameras should cover the action. However, a 'programme recording form' in the production file for the story held at the BBC Written Archives Centre says the titles were 36s. The CD version of the soundtrack from the story has a new, 'clean'

---

[10] Episode 2.

title theme, not the one as broadcast, but the titles on the older, cassette version last for 22s. So already there is conflict among the available sources, and we're not even into the story.

The camera script tells us that after the opening titles there were 52s of material recorded on film, comprising six individual shots:

**Ext. Airfield. Day**

**Shot 1**: ESTABLISHING SHOT of Airfield.

**Shot 2**: DOCTOR WHO and JAMIE hurrying towards a hangar.

**Shot 3**: Lorry emerging from hangar slowly and turning away. On the back of the lorry can be seen the Tardis, the Police Telephone Box, securely roped down.

On the side of the lorry is written the name of the firm:

'Leatherman'

**Shot 4**: C.U. DOCTOR WHO and JAMIE. Horrified reaction.

SUPER SLIDE: Title: 'The Evil of the Daleks'

**Shot 5**: Lorry still turning, disappearing down the side of the hangar.

**Shot 6**: DOCTOR WHO and JAMIE running towards hangar and disappearing lorry.

'Tele-snaps' – photographs taken of the episode as it was broadcast[11] – clearly show that the title of the story, 'BY DAVID WHITAKER' and 'EPISODE 1', were shown over the opening titles.

---

[11] See 'Doctor Who Photonovels: The Evil of the Daleks'.

That means the list of shots in the camera script is not exactly what appeared in the episode, but the description of them seems very specific, and it's possible the list was written after the sequence filmed on location had been edited, ready to be played in during studio recording.

Although the series was well established by this point, note that the lead character is referred to as 'DOCTOR WHO' in the script, as if Who is his surname. Today, the convention is that **Doctor Who** is the name of the series but the lead character is simply 'the Doctor'. Likewise, the convention now is to refer to the Doctor's spaceship as the 'TARDIS' – all capitals. These may seem minor concerns, but remind us that many conventions that we take for granted had not yet been established. What we now think of as the Doctor and TARDIS is not the same as when this episode was broadcast.

Even without dialogue the story quickly establishes what's at stake – the Doctor in pursuit of the TARDIS – whether or not we saw the previous story, *The Faceless Ones* (1967). While that story was set in – and filmed at – Gatwick Airport, the hangar seen in this episode was part of the BBC Outside Broadcasts and Transport Base on Kendall Avenue in west London. So the first shot in the camera script, establishing the airport, must have come from previously existing footage, and the most likely place is from material shot at Gatwick for *The Faceless Ones*. Perhaps it reused footage from episode 1 of that story, also used to establish the setting. If so, the opening short of *The Evil of the Daleks* still exists – because episode 1 of *The Faceless Ones* is held in the BBC archive. It would be nice to think so, but there's nothing in the surviving sources to confirm it.

The tele-snaps reveal how shots 2 and 3 were composed. The first shows a high shot looking down on the TARDIS on the back of the lorry, the cab moving out of shot off the bottom of frame. There's an expanse of pale grey car park behind the dark outline of the TARDIS. Presumably the lorry continued out of shot, taking the TARDIS with it and leaving the car park empty, perhaps to visually underline the Doctor's loss of his ship.

The high angle was achieved by filming from a crane on the back of a Land Rover, which can be seen in two of the five photographs taken by costume designer Sandra Reid – now Alexandra Tynan – and published in the fanzine *DWB* in 1991[12]. In one image we can see what's being filmed: the lorry, with the sign 'Leatherman' in white lettering on black, pulling out from the 'hangar' on the right. As per the script, we would have seen the lorry emerge from the hangar on the right-hand side of frame, proceed into the middle of shot and turn 90 degrees counter-clockwise before driving 'down' and out of frame.

Tynan's other four photographs seem to have been taken from roughly the same standing position, turning to watch the lorry and the pursuing Doctor and Jamie go past. From Tynan's five images, we could infer that the Doctor and Jamie chased after the lorry while being filmed from the crane – which is not the shot as described in the script.

However, the next tele-snap shows shot 3, no longer from the crane and with the lorry taking up most of the frame as it moves off

---

[12] 'Someone's Stolen the TARDIS!!'. *DWB: The Journal of British Telefantasy* #94, October 1991.

the right-hand edge. As indicated in the script, this gives the viewer a clear sight of the name 'Leatherman' on the side of the lorry. The Doctor and Jamie – running behind the lorry – don't know the name 'Leatherman' when Bob Hall mentions it later. That suggests they can't have been too close behind when the lorry turned 90 degrees.

In this tele-snap, the angle of the shot is almost identical to the three on-set images taken by Tynan showing the Doctor and Jamie, suggesting she stood close to the camera when she took her pictures. That means Tynan's three images and the tele-snap flow nicely when placed in sequence – as in fan reconstructions of the story – giving a better sense of this individual shot.

But the Doctor and Jamie are not mentioned in this shot in the camera script. The running order included with it says there were five shots, not six, in the sequence, so perhaps director Derek Martinus joined up shot 3 and shot 4: the lorry moved out of frame as the Doctor and Jamie hurried after it and, all in the same shot, came into close up so we'd see their horrified reactions. That's a more economical way of conveying the necessary detail for the story – but is it what was done? One of Tynan's photographs, used on the cover of *DWB*, seems to show the Doctor and Jamie slowing to a stop, exasperation on their faces – but we can't tell if that was being recorded or, if it was, whether it was part of the same shot or a separate one. There's no record of the remaining shots in this sequence.

We then cut from 16mm location film to the interior of the transport fuel office, recorded in Studio D of Lime Grove so with the distinctive warm, fluid tone of footage captured on videotape.

According to the camera script, this scene opened on a close-up of some unspecified object on some Dexion shelving – we don't know what the object was. The camera was then to crab left, looking through the Dexion shelving to find the character Bob Hall in medium close-up. Having established the setting, the Doctor and Jamie would enter from the upper part of frame, coming forward to join Hall in a close three-shot.

Once the Doctor introduced himself and asked Hall if he could help, the camera was to pan right to find a prop ladder in the foreground, reaching to the upper edge of frame. A tele-snap shows this arrangement: Hall on the left looking nervously at the Doctor, who is in the centre of shot with Jamie beside him – all three close together in the room full of boxes, a ladder standing against the edge of frame.

There are no further tele-snaps from this scene but we can follow the camera script: the same camera stayed on this three-shot as the Doctor interrogated Hall, then cut to a two-shot of the Doctor and Jamie as they worried about the TARDIS. There were a total of five separate camera shots. It's not a rapid, urgent sequence; rather Derek Martinus allows a disquieting tension to build.

We cut from this – Scene 1 in the script, as it's the first one recorded in studio – to more location film, with Kennedy lying in low grass listening to the Doctor's conversation on some kind of radio set. The next tele-snap shows a close-up of Kennedy with the device close to his face. He's clearly wearing an earpiece but on the soundtrack we, too, hear the Doctor's voice, slightly distorted by being overhead on the device. This is a simple way of conveying exactly what Kennedy is doing – i.e. eavesdropping – but it also makes us complicit in spying on the Doctor, raising the tension.

The script says that beside Kennedy are a paperback and a half-consumed packet of sandwiches, conveying, again without dialogue, that he's waited some time. The implication is that the TARDIS hasn't been taken by accident; it's some organised plot.

We cut between film footage of Kennedy and Scene 2 of the studio recording as the Doctor interrogates Hall and Kennedy listens in. Page six of the camera script is followed by 'New page 7', in which Kennedy speaks into his radio. The following tele-snap shows him doing so, in a medium close-up with trees behind him. Having spoken, the script tells us he lifts his binoculars to his eyes and watches the Doctor and Jamie. The subsequent tele-snap shows us this, a long shot of the Doctor and Jamie bordered with a black outline that's the convention for something seen through binoculars. Two further tele-snaps show us the end of this sequence, with Jamie and the Doctor beside the petrol pumps – in close-up and not seen through binoculars.

Even if Kennedy watches the Doctor and Jamie through binoculars, he can't be too far from them, so must be in the vicinity of the airport. But the script only specifies a 'field' and 'grass', making it easy for the production team to use a nondescript location at any convenient point in the schedule.

Scene 3 then begins, in the study of the antique shop run by the mysterious Edward Waterfield. It's a short scene, followed by a brief sequence filmed on location, before Scene 4 returns to the study of the antique shop. Apart from two pictures of the opening titles, off-air photographs taken by designer Chris Thompson begin with these scenes in the study, but we can't simply alternate between his pictures and the tele-snaps. Information in the camera scripts can help us work out the sequence.

First, a tele-snap shows a side view of Waterfield at his desk, holding a receiver device (on which he is talking to Kennedy). According to 'New page 8' of the camera script, Scene 3 began with a close-up of Waterfield's hands on the desk, one hand writing on paper before laying down the pen to lift the radio mic – the camera pulling out to show Waterfield, as in the tele-snap, by the time he starts speaking.

The next tele-snap shows Waterfield speaking into the radio but now from face on. According to the camera script, this new angle cut in on Waterfield's line 'I knew they would suspect him.' Waterfield doesn't use the receiver in Scene 4, so we can safely conclude that both tele-snaps are from Scene 3.

The episode then cut to the filmed sequence of the Doctor and Jamie hailing a taxi to pursue Bob Hall in his car. No images are known to survive from this sequence.

According to the script, Scene 4 began with a tracked-out close-up shot of Waterfield through a magnifying glass. A tele-snap shows this, the magnifying glass filling the middle of the lower half of the frame, obscuring Waterfield's mouth and nose as we look at him face on. After the knock on the door, the camera was to elevate and track out as Waterfield went to answer it, providing the first establishing shot of the room. That's what we see in the first of Chris Thompson's images: a wide shot of the room full of antiques, Waterfield with his back to us as he bends to unlock the double doors in the centre of the frame. We can see Waterfield from head to toe, but with his back to us it's not clear from this image – as it is in the script – that he's wearing Victorian clothes. Note that the dialogue doesn't refer to what he is wearing: it's a visual clue to him being out of his own time, bolstered by Waterfield's later, spoken, mix-up over guineas and pounds.

The tele-snap that follows is from a moment later: the same camera position but with the door now open. Waterfield has stepped back and to the right, and is in profile as he faces Perry. The next is a close two-shot of Perry and Waterfield as Perry admires an antique just off the left-hand edge of frame. The script says this is a clock on Waterfield's desk, but Waterfield's desk is visible on the far side of the room. The dialogue doesn't say 'clock', so Perry might be admiring something else.

Thompson's next photograph shows Perry in roughly the same position, but Waterfield some distance behind him, on the other side of his desk. This is almost identical to the next tele-snap, except Perry is bent a little lower to examine whatever antique is just out of shot, and Waterfield is slightly further left behind the desk – the suggestion being that after the previous tele-snap he moved right, off the edge of frame, and then came into shot again behind the desk.

Again, the next of Thompson's images is almost identical to the subsequent tele-snap, looking down on Perry as he seems to admire the room's chandelier, and it's difficult to tell which of the two images comes first. The last of Thompson's images from this scene still has Perry gazing upwards at the chandelier, but we can also see Waterfield standing behind his desk. Since that suggests the camera has pulled back and to the left since the previous two images, we can perhaps work out the order by comparing the position of the leg of Waterfield's desk to Perry's shoulder. In the tele-snap, the leg is some distance from Perry; in Thompson's similar image, Perry's arm just obscures the very end of the leg; in Thompson's next image the leg is completely behind him[13].

By the end of Scene 4, we're a quarter of the way into this first episode. We could continue in this vein, piecing together the story from the surviving sources, noting how it builds up suspense through a mixture of spoken and visual clues. But we're missing something important. This is contemporary London, a place of Dexion shelves, taxis and petrol pumps. The more ordinary and mundane the details, the stranger the whole thing must have seemed to viewers at the time.

## Here and Now

At this point in **Doctor Who**'s history, visits to contemporary Earth were rare: after the first episode ('An Unearthly Child', *An Unearthly Child* episode 1 (1963)), the next time the TARDIS lands in what is apparently the present day is 'Planet of Giants' (*Planet of Giants* episode 1 (1964)); even there, the Doctor and his friends are miniaturised so the everyday world becomes as strange as anywhere they've been in time and space. When the Doctor's companions Ian and Barbara return home to 1960s London in 'The Planet of Decision' (*The Chase* episode 6 (1965)), they do so in a Dalek time machine; the Doctor and TARDIS don't go with them. In 'The Feast of Steven' and 'Volcano' (*The Daleks' Master Plan*

---

[13] See comparison at Guerrier, Simon, 'Off Air Images from *The Evil of the Daleks*'.

episodes 7 (1965) and 8 (1966)) and 'Bell of Doom' (*The Massacre* episode 4 (1966)), the TARDIS stops briefly in the present day, but with little chance for the Doctor to interact with contemporary surroundings. And then a change of production team sees a major shift in thinking.

The first episode of *The War Machines* was broadcast on 25 June 1966 – the 123rd episode of **Doctor Who**, more than two and a half years since the series began. *The War Machines* is the first full story set on and interacting with contemporary Earth, a statement of intent from new producer Innes Lloyd. 'I wanted the kind of adventure stories you could relate to in everyday life,' he later said[14].

A year after *The War Machines*, another full story – *The Faceless Ones* – and the first episode and a half of *The Evil of the Daleks* were also set on contemporary Earth, apparently all on the same day. Lloyd also phased out stories set in the past where the Doctor was mostly a passive observer of historical events – the last of these was *The Highlanders* (1966-67). *The Evil of the Daleks* would offer a new, more engaging formula for stories set in history.

Many of the Lloyd-produced **Doctor Who** stories set in the future are not too distant from the audience's own time: *The Tenth Planet* (1966) is set in 1986 – a relatively short jump forward – and *The Underwater Menace* (1967) takes place in about 1970. The story after that, *The Moonbase* (1967), is set 100 years later in 2070 – just as the middle section of *The Evil of the Daleks* is set 100 years

---

[14] 'Innes Lloyd'. *Doctor Who Magazine* (DWM) Winter Special, 1983.

in the past, in both cases periods that almost feel within reach. *The Moonbase* also mirrored real events of the time: Apollo 1, intended to be the first flight in the programme that would ultimately land people on the Moon, had been scheduled to launch on 21 February 1967 – in between broadcasts of *The Moonbase* episodes 2 and 3.

Making **Doctor Who** more contemporary proved very effective, and the series has frequently visited the present day or near future ever since. Of course, there was a practical advantage, as designer Chris Thompson explains:

> 'It was easier because the BBC had all these pieces of scenery with doors, windows and bits of walls that you could order. You'd get them delivered to the workshop and then you could start putting your own ideas on to things that already existed, so you weren't starting completely from scratch. That was easier than science fiction, because there wouldn't have been much in stock at the BBC stores up at Alexandra Palace. So the money didn't stretch as far.'

As science fiction was rarer than drama set in the present, designers had more experience of creating a credible 'now':

> 'Oh yeah, I did lots of [police series] **Z Cars** and things like that, which was all lock-ups and garages, so you knew how to make them look.'

That said, the Tricolour coffee bar in *The Evil of the Daleks* was more unusual:

'It was all bright red, white and blue. Unfortunately, I've never seen any colour photos of it. But that was something I really enjoyed designing. I went to places like that then.'[15]

The name of the bar is a reference to the national flag of France, adopted during the revolution of 1789. But this isn't a place of dour history: indeed, there's a joke made of Jamie – himself from the 18th century – being so out-of-place and boggling at the girls in mini-skirts. This bar offers revolutionary newness: young people in the latest fashions, listening to the latest chart hits. The choice of name conveys something else, too. The modernist or 'mod' look had been around since the 1950s, but historian Dominic Sandbrook identifies a second wave beginning in 1964: 'The whole point was to cultivate a look of "effortless" Continental sophistication.'[16]

More specifically, between 1968 and 1970, writer David Whitaker provided an entry for himself to the reference book series *Contemporary Authors*:

> 'I travel widely in Europe, particularly France and Italy. [I am] fascinated by tradition and historic societies influencing each new generation, and the essential differences between this and the developing of newer countries, which approach

---

[15] Thompson, Chris, interview with author, 11 July 2016.
[16] Dominic Sandbrook, *White Heat: A History of Britain in the Swinging Sixties*, p206.

30

national and international problems without the pressures of the past dictating or advising their decisions.'[17]

Is the Tricolour a nod to the way the past informs the present? Or perhaps it's an in-joke about **Doctor Who**, as Whitaker had been story editor on the Doctor's visit to revolutionary France in *The Reign of Terror* (1964). The horrors seen in that story are now merely a backdrop for girls in miniskirts.

It's a cliché to speak of the mid-1960s as the province solely of the trendy and young. Of course, the Tricolour is no more representative of the time than the other contemporary settings: the hangars of the airport, the warehouse and antique shop. In fact, as we'll see, an antique shop full of Victoriana is just as mid-60s as the trendy bar.

Yet the opening of *The Evil of the Daleks* is striking for more than being set in the present day. For the first time since the series began, the Doctor and his companion – as well as the audience watching – begin the story already knowing where they are in time and space, rather than having to deduce this by exploring outside the TARDIS[18]. In fact, though, the episode is not quite set in the present but almost a year in the past. The reason why shows how the intentions of the production team – such as to make the series

---

[17] The entry I have for David Whitaker is from a photocopy made by fan Gary Hopkins while in correspondence with Whitaker in the late 1970s.

[18] *The Edge of Destruction* (1964) is set almost entirely inside the TARDIS, but in the first episode the Doctor and his companions still try to work out where they have 'crashed'.

more contemporary – were tempered by practical considerations as episodes were made.

## The Revolving Door of the TARDIS

The production team on **Doctor Who** needed *The Evil of the Daleks* to do three things. David Whitaker was asked to introduce a potential new companion – a character we'll discuss in the next chapter. He had to write the Daleks out of **Doctor Who**, which we'll examine in Chapter 3. But when he was commissioned in January 1967, the first two episodes also needed to be set in the present day so as to write out companions Ben and Polly – who don't even appear in the story as broadcast.

Anneke Wills and Michael Craze – playing Polly and Ben – had originally been issued with contracts on 26 May 1966 for four **Doctor Who** serials, taking them to the end of *The Power of the Daleks* (1966). On 2 November, a few days after the recording of episode 2 of that story, Craze was contracted for three further stories – *The Highlanders*, *The Underwater Menace* and *The Moonbase* – as was Wills, the following day.

However, *The Highlanders* introduced a new character, Jamie McCrimmon, played by Frazer Hines. The production team had always considered Jamie as a potential companion – Hines's contract, dated 2 November, included an option for him to appear in three further stories – but scenes filmed on location on 14 November included the TARDIS leaving without him. The decision to retain Hines must have been made soon after that, as the scene was reshot on 21 November, this time with Polly leading Jamie into the TARDIS. The option for Hines to appear in the next story, *The Underwater Menace*, was taken up on 13 December – the day before he started location filming on that story. As Hines remembered:

> 'The scripts for that had already been written before they took me on. So they simply gave me some of Ben's lines, making them sound more Highlands than London.'

In fact, the production team were considering Jamie taking Ben's place altogether. On 12 December Wills was contracted for a further 12 episodes after *The Moonbase*. This covered the four episodes of *The Macra Terror* (1967) and then, had they both remained four-part stories, what became *The Faceless Ones* and *The Evil of the Daleks*. But Craze's contract was not extended at the same time. Hines recalls:

> 'I kept my head down. I was the new boy, I just learnt my lines and got on with it. But Mike must have been aware. I know how I'd have felt if I'd been doing the show for a year and they brought in a new guy.'[19]

In her autobiography, *Self Portrait* (2007), Wills recalls being summoned to Lloyd's office and asked to stay on with Hines instead of Craze:

> 'It has been such fun and such hard work. But I think that if I go on, I might become reliant on the £60 a week and I may never get out of it. Also, there is the stigma of being

---

[19] Hines, Frazer, interview with author, 3 August 2016.

typecast. And I want to be home again with my children. So I decide to leave with Mike.'[20]

She says now:

> 'I remember thinking two things. First, "What rotters! They're getting rid of Ben! Well, I'll go with him!" And also I thought it was a good excuse. The money and security were nice, but I thought there were other things I should be doing. The Royal Shakespeare Company was waiting for me – at least, that's what I thought.'[21]

Meanwhile, time off over Christmas 1966 meant a week lost from the production schedule, so the first episode of *The Underwater Menace* was recorded in studio on 7 January 1967, just one week ahead of broadcast. This tight turnaround continued for more than six months – up to *The Evil of the Daleks* episode 7, recorded on 24 June and broadcast on 1 July.

This and problems with scripts seem to have forced Innes Lloyd and Gerry Davis to abandon their plan of having four-part stories. On 2 January, the story that became *The Faceless Ones* was expanded from four episodes to six, and *The Evil of the Daleks* from four to seven. This meant Wills was now contracted up to episode 2 of the latter, which – since she'd turned down the chance to stay on – would now be her final episode. Though Craze was still only contracted up to the end of *The Moonbase*, the intention was clearly that he would leave at the same time: in David Whitaker's

---

[20] Wills, Anneke, *Self Portrait: My Journey As An Actress, Wife And Mother In The Swinging Sixties*, p231.
[21] Wills, Anneke, interview with author, 20 July 2016.

two-page breakdown for *The Evil of the Daleks*, dated 4 January, Polly and Ben are left behind in contemporary London when the Doctor and Jamie are lured back in time.

Hines's contract was extended on 16 January. On 24 January, Whitaker was contracted to write the seven episodes of *The Evil of the Daleks*, with a delivery date of 1 March. Craze's contract was extended up to episode 2 of that story on 27 January. Whitaker delivered his script for the first episode, featuring Ben and Polly, on 8 February.

That script no longer seems to exist. The BBC Written Archives Centre holds the breakdown of 4 January as well as the camera scripts used when the story was recorded. The breakdown is a very brief summary, not even in full sentences, with the whole of episode 2 detailed in 31 words. As a result, we don't know what originally would have happened to Ben and Polly. Presumably they helped the Doctor and Jamie in looking for the TARDIS, and got as far as Waterfield's antique shop – which, the breakdown says, the Doctor finds at the end of episode 1. But would they have seen their friends disappearing back in time or got to say goodbye? In the broadcast version, the last line spoken in 1966 is Perry's remark to the policeman: 'Oh, they seem to have disappeared.'[22] The haunting possibility is that's how it would have been for Ben and Polly, the disappearance of their friends ever a lingering mystery.

The same day that Whitaker delivered his first script – perhaps even because of it – memos in the production file record a major change in what was wanted. Ben and Polly would now leave in the

---

[22] *The Evil of the Daleks* episode 2.

previous story. On 13 February, the BBC confirmed to Whitaker's agent, Beryl Vertue, that Whitaker would receive an additional 50% of his fee for the first two episodes because of the substantial work required by the new brief.

Wills and Craze left **Doctor Who** after recording episode 2 of *The Faceless Ones*, appearing again only at the end of episode 6 in a scene filmed on location weeks before studio recording. We'll address why in a moment.

The farewell scene was filmed at Gatwick Airport on 13 March, after last-minute revisions to the rehearsal script were made that morning[23]. From what we can deduce from surviving paperwork, these changes included Ben now remarking on the date, amazed because 'July the 20th 1966 is when it all began.'[24] The implication is that it's the same date that he and Polly first entered the TARDIS in episode 4 of *The War Machines*, so they can return home 'as if we've never been away'.

It's a neat way of returning him and Polly home without being asked awkward questions about where they have been and why Ben – a sailor – missed his ship. But it raises questions, too.

The first episode and a half of *The Evil of the Daleks* follow on directly from this scene, so does it take place on the same day as the events of both *The Faceless Ones* and *The War Machines*? If so, London was visited by Dalek agents, faceless alien Chameleons and tank-like mobile computers on 20 July, and it's odd nobody

---

[23] Pixley, Andrew, 'Trouble in Store', *Nothing at the End of the Lane #4*.
[24] *The Faceless Ones* episode 6.

mentions this fact on screen. Perhaps only a few people outside those directly involved in the events of *The Faceless Ones* would have known about the Chameleons, but the War Machines rampaged through London in broad daylight, and we see TV news reports about them. So why does no one in *The Evil of the Daleks* – at the airport, in the Tricolour or when the Doctor meets Perry – mention them?

One explanation is that *The War Machines* takes place over two days, and it's possible the final scene, when Ben and Polly first enter the TARDIS, is set at least another day after the Doctor defeats the computers[25]. In episode 1, we're told the nation's computer systems are due to come under the control of the central computer, WOTAN, on 'Monday, July the 16th'. WOTAN is just about to seize control at the end of episode 4, broadcast on 16 July 1966 – a Saturday. So most of the episode takes place on the same date if not the same day of the week as broadcast, but the final scene is set four days in the future.

Three days after the filming of Ben and Polly's farewell scene, on 16 March David Whitaker delivered scripts for the first five episodes of *The Evil of the Daleks*. He doesn't seem to have known that the first episode and a half were now set a year in the past: even the camera scripts give the date for the Victorian part of his story as 1867 – not 1866 as broadcast – suggesting the Doctor and Jamie

---

[25] An unspecified amount of time has clearly passed. Polly is wearing different clothes, and the message she brings from the Doctor's previous companion, Dodo, is that Dodo would like to 'stay in London'. Last we heard (in episode 2), Dodo was at Sir Charles Summer's 'house in the country' – that is, outside the city.

travelled back 100 years from 1967. The 1867 date would continue to appear in published synopses of the story long after broadcast.

Wills and Craze were paid to the end of their contracts – that is, for five episodes they didn't appear in. This seems to have been justified on the basis that the writers of *The Faceless Ones*, David Ellis and Malcolm Hulke, could devote more screen time to the potential replacement for Polly, a young woman initially called Mary Dawson, then Cleopatra 'Cleo' Briggs, and finally, by 23 February, Samantha Briggs.

Whitaker had also been tasked with including a potential new companion in *The Evil of the Daleks* but it seems Samantha was producer Innes Lloyd's preferred choice. She was, like Polly (and Dodo before her) a fashionable, modern young woman from the present day, easy for the audience to relate to – in line with Lloyd's plans for the series. Samantha is also a lively, funny character. Lloyd wanted to '[m]ake her a very tough character, very strong-willed, so we would have an equivalent to those girls in [adventure series] **The Avengers**.'[26]

Cast as Samantha was Pauline Collins. Her first day in studio was 8 April, to record episode 2 of the story. Perhaps it was then that Lloyd asked her about becoming the new companion, and perhaps he suggested she have time to think about it – the schedule gave her the following two days off. The production team seem to have thought she'd say 'yes', given what happened next.

---

[26] Rigelsford, 'Producing Who: Innes Lloyd'. DWM #180.

On the Monday – 10 April – director Derek Martinus auditioned six women for the part of Victoria in *The Evil of the Daleks*. Initially Denise Buckley was offered the part:

> 'I was cast for that one story, for six episodes. But sometime after I was cast it was decided that the character would become the new regular and I simply didn't fit the brief. The producers wanted her to be small and cute!'[27]

Production assistant Timothy Combe recalls:

> 'I know Denise, but I don't remember this. Patrick Troughton wasn't particularly tall, and nor is Frazer, so there might have been a worry about how the three of them would look in shot. But to be honest it sounds like Innes Lloyd to me, and story editor Peter Bryant. "No, she doesn't look like a **Doctor Who** girl – they have to be small!"'[28]

The recasting was confirmed by Lloyd on 13 April in two memos: one confirming that Buckley would not now be used but that she would be paid in full; the other confirming the casting of Deborah Watling. Clearly, between 10 and 13 April, Pauline Collins turned down the offer to stay on in the series. 'I don't like to stay in anything for too long a time,' she explained to DWM in 1994. 'I have a low boredom threshold.'[29] In 2012, she was more emphatic

---

[27] Buckley, Denise, interview with author, 4 August 2016.

[28] Combe, Timothy, interview with author, 25 July 2016.

[29] Townsend, Anthony, 'Acting the Part: Pauline Collins'. DWM #212.

about her decision. 'I thought it was like a prison sentence,' she told *The Guardian*[30].

With just over a week before the start of location filming for *The Evil of the Daleks* on 20 April, things then had to move quickly. According to Combe, 'the team knew they needed a new **Doctor Who** girl and it was up between Jo Rowbottom and Debbie Watling.'[31] Watling won the part of Victoria, and Rowbottom was cast in the supporting role of Mollie Dawson, her contract issued on 11 April, suggesting all this happened just a day after Buckley had been cast. Perhaps that haste explains why the production team saw two women they already knew: Rowbottom had previously worked for director Derek Martinus in the musical comedy *State of Emergency* at the Pembroke Theatre, Croydon, in 1962; Watling had already met with Lloyd to discuss another potential role in **Doctor Who** (in her autobiography, she denies that this was for the part of Polly, as other sources suggest)[32].

If Collins had stayed, the scripts for *The Evil of the Daleks* would all have had to be rewritten to include her – and with **Doctor Who** now recording just one week before broadcast, there was no way the schedule could be pushed back to allow extra time for rewrites. In the next chapter, we'll consider what Samantha's role might have been in the story.

---

[30] Hattenstone, Simon, 'Pauline Collins: From Shirley Valentine to Dustin Hoffman'.

[31] Rigelsford, Adrian, 'Interview: Tim Combe'. DWM 10th Anniversary Special.

[32] Watling, Deborah, with Paul WT Ballard, *Daddy's Girl: The Autobiography*, p45.

In the meantime, the scripts **didn't** need to be rewritten, and were all set to go into production.

## Crew of *Evil*

The production team were wary of hiring Derek Martinus again after he directed *The Tenth Planet* in late 1966. The first episode of that story had massively exceeded the budget – at £4,835, it was more than £1,500 over the already more-than-usual amount allotted to cover the pre-filming, eye-catching sets and costumes for the new monsters, the Cybermen[33]. Innes Lloyd reported his concerns about Martinus's handling of the production to Shaun Sutton, the BBC's Head of Serials, but admitted in a memo dated 30 January 1967 that the director couldn't be blamed for all the problems on the story. (It was hardly his fault that illness meant lead actor William Hartnell was hastily written out of episode 3.)

Having talked to story editors Gerry Davis and Peter Bryant, Lloyd told Sutton they were prepared to let Martinus direct *The Evil of the Daleks* but asked for a first-rate production assistant, production secretary and assistant floor manager to support him. The suggestion is that Martinus wasn't terribly organised. His daughter Charlotta Martinus observes:

> 'My Mum talked about how she had to organise him, too. He'd miss flights and never know where his glasses were, and because he couldn't remember things he'd be for ever

---

[33] Pixley, Andrew, 'Daleks: Invasion USA 1967AD'. DWM #406.

writing things down in little notepads. He did have that slightly chaotic element to him.'[34]

Tim Combe was assigned to him as production assistant:

> 'Derek was a lovely fellow but he did need to be looked after a bit. **Doctor Who** was always a programme that challenged people.'

Combe trained as an actor and joined the BBC in 1961, working as assistant floor manager and then production assistant in the serials department. He'd already been production assistant on two **Doctor Who** stories – *The Keys of Marinus* and *The Reign of Terror* (both 1964).

> 'The production assistant was really the assistant director and production manager. In the studio recordings, I was in charge of the studio floor while the director was up in the gallery. I would also go out and find filming locations, plan the schedules and generally take charge of things. I kept control of all location filming, and I was the person people came to if there were any queries or matters of discipline.'[35]

On 3 March, designer Chris Thompson was assigned to the production after James Bould, manager of scenic design resources, had to reassign the original designer, Colin Shaw. Thompson recalls:

> 'I don't know what happened there. But it's pretty exceptional that they gave me the production. I was only 23, which was very young. Producers and directors usually had a

---

[34] Martinus, Charlotta, interview with author, 7 September 2016.
[35] Combe, interview with author.

choice, to some extent, of who worked on their productions. Given the pressures and everything, they were usually conservative and wanted people they'd worked with before. And without sounding too harsh, I was never too enthralled about working on **Doctor Who** – I mean, it was fine, but I knew it would be a lot of work!'

One factor in his favour was that he'd worked as an assistant on several previous **Doctor Who** stories:

'I was assistant to Raymond Cusick on *The Rescue* and *The Romans* [both 1965] and another Dalek one[36]. And I assisted John Wood on *The Celestial Toymaker* [1966]. That wasn't just sitting in the office drawing or being a general dogsbody. I was on the studio floor with them, getting it all done. So I knew what it involved.'[37]

So: the producers wanted to make **Doctor Who** more contemporary and real, but their plans had to be tempered by practical concerns, such as the changing cast and how feasibly things could be filmed or recorded. An experienced crew would help deliver on the ambition. But there's another big influence on *The Evil of the Daleks* – the time in which it was made. A story about a Victorian antique shop couldn't have been more of its day.

---

[36] From Thompson's memories of working with Jean Marsh, that must have been *The Daleks' Master Plan* (1965-6).
[37] Thompson, interview with author.

## Genuine Reproductions

On 25 January 1967, two days before Whitaker was formally commissioned to write *The Evil of the Daleks*, the writer John Fowles noted in his diary that he'd started work on a new novel[38]. Although set 100 years before in 1867, *The French Lieutenant's Woman* was 'a distinctly "postmodern" novel, in which the narrator draws explicit parallels with the world of the 1960s.'[39] He completed the first draft in October, and the novel was published in 1969. Fowles' diaries don't record whether he watched *The Evil of the Daleks*, let alone if it influenced his novel.

On 31 January 1967, four days after Whitaker was commissioned to write his scripts, John Lennon was in Sevenoaks where he 'wandered into an antiques shop and picked up a Victorian circus poster advertising "the last night but three" of a show put on by some travelling tumblers in Rochdale in 1843.' That poster became the basis for the Beatles' song, 'Being for the Benefit of Mr Kite!', recorded in February and March. In post-production, Lennon asked producer George Martin 'for a "fairground" [effect] wherein one could smell the sawdust'; Martin responded to this brief 'using harmonium, harmonicas, and a tape of Victorian steam organs and calliopes cut up and edited into a kaleidoscopic wash.'[40] This new and yet Victorian song was released to the public as part of the album *Sgt. Pepper's Lonely Hearts Club Band* on 1 June – five days after viewers had seen the Doctor and Jamie transported 100 years

---

[38] Fowles, John, ed Charles Drazin, *John Fowles: The Journals Volume 2* p27.
[39] Sandbrook, *White Heat*, p448.
[40] MacDonald, Ian, *Revolution in the Head*, pp237-8.

back in time. Another song on the album, 'Lucy in the Sky with Diamonds', was partially inspired by a chapter in Lewis Carroll's 1871 novel *Through the Looking-Glass, and What Alice Found There*[41]. The title track was also influenced by antique items on sale: '[Paul] McCartney was thinking of the period fashion then on sale in shops like I Was Lord Kitchener's Valet and Granny Takes a Trip.'[42]

The Beatles weren't **only** drawing from Victorian influences – like **Doctor Who**, they drew ideas from a great range of sources. But as Dominic Sandbrook argues, Peter Blake's cover for *Sgt. Pepper* 'nicely suited the contemporary fashion for Victorian revivalism.'[43] That fashion could be seen in London's Carnaby Street which 'teemed with fashionable establishments', among them 'Gear, a patriotic knick-knack shop selling tatty Victorian memorabilia and jewellery.'[44] Its patrons included Frazer Hines[45]. On the Kings Road, Granny Takes a Trip offered for sale Victorian bustles and feather boas among its stock of 'everything that would seem totally outdated and absurd.'[46]

Such clothes could be worn at the new discotheques, where patrons danced to music played either live or from records – just as in the Tricolour in *The Evil of the Daleks*. Again there was often a dash of Victoriana in such places: the Pickwick in Great Newport

---

[41] Sandbrook, *White Heat*, p438.

[42] MacDonald, *Revolution in the Head*, p233.

[43] Sandbrook, *White Heat*, p74.

[44] Sandbrook, *White Heat*, p249.

[45] Cook, Benjamin, 'The DWM Interview: Great Scot'. DWM #458.

[46] Sandbrook, *White Heat*, p452.

Street, which 'epitomised the spirit of Swinging London' and was 'closely associated with showbusiness figures like John Barry, Terence Stamp and Michael Caine', 'was designed in a style described as "Victorian whimsy."'[47] At the Scotch of St James, also patronised by Hines, 'the disc jockey was hidden inside a 19th-century coach next to the dance floor.'[48]

As well as this playful mash-up of Victoriana with fashion, pop music and the stars of film and TV, the mid-1960s also saw more serious re-engagement with the 19th century. Steven Marcus's *The Other Victorians: A Study of Sexuality and Pornography in Mid-Nineteenth-Century England* (1966) was not the first study of Victorian attitudes to sex but its psychoanalytic approach proved very influential. Matthew Sweet says in *Inventing the Victorians* (2002), that '[m]ost subsequent treatments of Victorian sexuality have been written with reference to' Marcus's idea of a strict duality, where:

> 'aspects of the Victorians' sex lives which could not be accommodated within the institution of monogamous marriage were part of some clandestine nightscape; an underworld into which the Victorians policed every subversive element.'[49]

Such duality is at the heart of **The Forsyte Saga** (1967), the first 11 of whose 26 episodes are set in Victorian times (the death of Victoria is announced in episode 12). The series was met with

---

[47] Sandbrook, *White Heat*, p262.
[48] Sandbrook, *White Heat*, p264.
[49] Sweet, Matthew, *Inventing the Victorians*, p209.

acclaim when first broadcast on BBC Two in 1967, and watched by a third of the country when repeated on BBC One the following year. Dominic Sandbrook examines how it was discussed in the press: a letter from one Mr Boydall of Leeds, published in *The Times* on 6 March 1969, raged against contemporary politics and 'the sight and sound of scruffy teenagers and students and kitchen sink drama! [...] No wonder we are happy to escape for 45 minutes each week into a world of elegance and good manners.'[50] But what really hooked viewers were the murky goings-on beneath that respectable veneer: adultery, reckless gambling, and a sex scandal that lands the daughter of an aristocrat in court, to the embarrassment of a prominent MP. In clips from **Talkback** (1967) and **Late Night Line-Up** (1964-72) included on the series' 2004 DVD release, the debate is largely about whose side to take after the scene in episode 6 in which austere Victorian Soames Forsyte rapes his wife Irene.

**The Forsyte Saga** was adapted and produced by Donald Wilson. As Head of Serials at the BBC until 1965, Wilson co-created **Doctor Who** and appointed David Whitaker – who'd worked in his department since 1957 – as its first story editor. Whitaker's then-wife, June Barry, appeared as June Forsyte in 16 episodes of the drama. On 3 January, the day before Whitaker submitted his outline for *The Evil of the Daleks*, she was in studio to record the episode *Conflict*. Is it too much to think that his wife's starring role in a Victorian-set drama might have influenced Whitaker in writing the first ever Victorian-set **Doctor Who** story?

---

[50] Quoted in Sandbrook, *White Heat*, pp446-7.

Tim Combe, who knew Whitaker and Barry personally, thinks not:

> 'David was a good writer and he had a very interesting mind.
> I'm sure it was all him. That script for *The Evil of the Daleks*
> was quite ahead of its time, the way he thought it through.
> How he switched between the Victorian and the science
> fiction.'[51]

If **The Forsyte Saga** didn't have a direct influence, there are links
between the two productions. John Bailey plays Waterfield,
introduced in episode 1 of *The Evil of the Daleks*, first broadcast on
20 May 1967. Later that same evening, Bailey could be seen as
louche artist Aubrey Greene in episode 20 of **The Forsyte Saga** –
the third of four appearances. His first was in an episode broadcast
on 29 April, when he'd already been cast as Waterfield – he was
sent the scripts for *The Evil of the Daleks* on 20 April and contracted
on the 24th. So director Derek Martinus can't have seen him in **The
Forsyte Saga**, but perhaps he had an eye on the production of such
a prestigious series. (Dalek operator John Scott Martin also appears
in **The Forsyte Saga**, as does Christopher Benjamin, who Martinus
considered for the part of Toby.)

There's a fun scene in Bailey's first episode of **The Forsyte Saga**
when, some time in the early 1920s, the aged Soames declares that
'the world reached its highest point in the 80s.' Bailey – as Greene
– fondly mocks this statement: 'I was too young to remember, but I
suppose you all believed in God and drove about in diligences?'
Soames corrects him on modes of transport and illustrates what
the period was like by telling an uncharacteristically romantic

---

[51] Combe, interview with author.

anecdote. But Soames's daughter assumes that her father has invented the story, and Greene agrees it has 'shades' of GA Henty's historical adventures[52]. Despite Soames's protestations, the Victorian period has become a kind of fiction – and it's possible even he is complicit in constructing the narrative. The scene marks a clear divide between the generations: the young can no more understand the world Soames is from than he can make sense of the 1920s slang used by Greene. In episode 1 of *The Evil of the Daleks*, Bailey plays a Victorian in the same position: he needs Perry to explain the word 'dicey'.

This divide between the Victorians and the generation that followed them perhaps explains what happened in the mid-1960s. The Victorians weren't being rediscovered, as such – they had never been out of view. 'For the first two or three decades of my life I met many old people who had been alive during the reign of Victoria, or who could share the memories of their parents' generation,' says AN Wilson, who was born in 1950:

> 'When I went up to Oxford in 1969 there were at least two pairs of spinster sisters, the Misses Butler and the Misses Deneke, who could remember tea parties with Lewis Carroll [...] Mine is the last, too, of the generations which can remember the physical details of Victorian life surviving. The waiting-rooms in British Railways stations in the 1950s were still gaslit. Old ladies in my childhood still clutched reticules;

---

[52] **The Forsyte Saga**: *The White Monkey*.

their cream-jugs were still covered with slightly cheesy beaded cloths.'[53]

For many in the 1950s, 'Victorian' was a pejorative term. It had become so even by 1918, when Lytton Strachey – born in 1880 – published *Eminent Victorians*, which Matthew Sweet refers to as a 'poison-pen letter to the past'[54]. By the 1950s and 1960s, new legislation was being proposed on issues such as divorce, abortion and homosexuality, to do away with Victorian – and therefore bad – law[55]. New housing blocks and estates were being built in modern, brutalist style to replace Victorian – and therefore bad – terraces[56].

There was no respite even for buildings of historical interest. Euston station had been built in 1837, the year Victoria ascended the throne and at the dawn of the age of the train. Its entrance gateway, the 22-metre high 'Euston Arch', was the largest Doric propylaeum ever built. Both were demolished in 1961-62 to make way for a new, larger building on more modernist lines.

As Sandbrook points out, faults with such modernist buildings and estates made them increasingly unpopular as the 1960s wore on. The destruction of the buildings at Euston also shocked many people, who realised they didn't want to sweep away the past. The Victorian Society, which held its first meeting in 1958, had failed to garner enough public support to prevent the demolition at Euston,

---

[53] Wilson, AN, *The Victorians*, p3.
[54] Sweet, *Inventing the Victorians*, ppxvi-xvii.
[55] Sandbrook, *White Heat*, p478.
[56] Sandbrook, *White Heat*, p626.

but by 1967 it had enough backing to save St Pancras station, which was formally listed on 1 November[57].

So there was a thawing in the disdain for all things Victorian, at least in some quarters. At the same time, genuine Victorians – people born before 1901 – were dying off and there seems, because of the divide, to have been little interest from their immediate descendants in keeping their clothes and possessions. Antique and second-hand shops were flooded with Victoriana, so it was offered for sale relatively cheaply. That made it accessible.

Just as the generation that followed the Victorians dismissed Victorian values, they found themselves at odds with the young people of the 1960s. 'I will not have Victorian junk in my flat,' Andrew Lloyd Webber was told by his grandmother, born in 1898, when he asked to borrow £50 to buy the unframed canvas of *Flaming June* by Frederic, Lord Leighton, on sale in a shop on the Fulham Road:

> 'In my grandmother's lifetime [John William Waterhouse's] paintings could scarcely be given away [and] there is a famous story that a certain Alma-Tadema painting was found chucked in a builder's skip. Its owner had kept the frame, thinking it more valuable [...] Of course, I was partly egged on by the vehemence of my peers' abuse of my various causes célèbres [but] as I began to have the good fortune to succeed in musical theatre, I inevitably wanted to form an art collection. The area of art that I knew something

[57] Sandbrook, *White Heat*, pp634-6.

about was Victorian and, importantly for me, it was affordable.'[58]

Lloyd Webber collected Victorian art specifically but, as we saw, in the fashionable shops and discotheques, Victorian clothes and artefacts were often bought as part of a mix of styles and historical periods to create jarring juxtapositions: Victoriana incongruously sitting with the achingly new.

The central premise of adventure serial **Adam Adamant Lives!** (1966-67) is that the dashing young hero adventuring through London is from the same period as his antique clothes – he was born in 1867. In Michael Reeves' film *The Sorcerers*, released in November 1967, Mike Roscoe (Ian Ogilvy) is a young man working in an antique shop full of Victoriana. An old married couple live vicariously through his experience, compelling him to go to nightclubs and forcing him to murder. The husband is played by horror star Boris Karloff, who was born in 1887, so Ogilvy goes a stage further than fashionable clothes: he's out clubbing with a real Victorian inside his head. **Doctor Who** having a real Victorian running a modern antique shop, taking orders from a Dalek, was entirely of the moment.

And then there's the music.

## Space Walk

On 12 June 1967, two days after the broadcast of episode 4 of *The Evil of the Daleks*, Queen Elizabeth II attended the premiere of the new **James Bond** film, *You Only Live Twice*. If she'd listened

---

[58] 'Andrew's Collection'.

carefully, she might have recognised the voice of Frazer Hines among the villains[59].

But there's another connection to *The Evil of the Daleks*. In the film's opening scene, an American space capsule in orbit round Earth is captured by another spacecraft, all to John Barry's lush orchestral cue, 'Space Walk.' The film's score was recorded in April and May at CTS studios in Bayswater, and photographs show violinist Alex Firman in the middle of the front row[60]. On 9 and 25 May, Firman was at Riverside Studios recording Dudley's Simpson's music for *The Evil of the Daleks*.

Barry's distinctive sound directly influenced the score for a later Patrick Troughton **Doctor Who** story set on present-day Earth – Don Harper's music for *The Invasion* (1968). Mark Ayres, a composer and sound designer who has studied the music used in **Doctor Who**, says:

> 'Harper was being terribly contemporary and he'd obviously seen what John Barry was doing with something like *The Ipcress File* [1965]. But Dudley's influences are less obvious. He wouldn't say, "I want to make it sound like John Barry." He'd work out what worked for the story. From his very first score for **Doctor Who**, *Planet of Giants* [1964], he basically went, "I've got giants and little people, so I'll use piccolo and bassoon." On *Evil*, in that first episode, you can perhaps hear

---

[59] 'I dubbed Japenese [sic] villains at the end of Bond movie "[Yo]u only live twice"' (Hines, Frazer. Tweet posted 12:10pm, 15 April 2013.)
[60] 'Photos YOLT recording (2)'.

the influence of 60s beat music – which is John Barry and of its time. But he didn't use a beat combo to do it; it's a little orchestra and eight players.'[61]

Alec Firman was the 'fixer', responsible for hiring the players. Session guitarist Vic Flick, who played alongside Firman on several Barry recordings, recalls that 'all the contractors, or fixers, in the recording industry at that time were violin players', and that the most powerful of them – including Firman – oversaw 'the great majority of the recording, television and radio work that was going on in London and, to a less extent, in the provinces.'[62]

Some 22m of music was recorded for episodes 1 to 3 at the session on 9 May, with a marimba, xylophone and vibraphone hired for the occasion. On 17 May, Firman was paid an additional sum to cover 'doublings', suggesting musicians played more than one instrument or part, to increase the body of the sound – a concern of Simpson's, as we'll see.

On a film, music was often recorded to fit footage already recorded and edited, but technology didn't allow for that in TV. 'In those days, you [couldn't] take a video home to study it,' Simpson recalled. 'They['d] just tell you what [the story was] all about.'"[63] Mark Ayres explains:

---

[61] Ayres, Mark, interview with author, 8 August 2016.
[62] Flick, Vic, *Guitarman: From James Bond to the Beatles and Beyond*, pp52, p311.
[63] Dudley Simpson, 'The Doctor's Composer' (extra on the 2009 DVD of *The War Games* (1969)).

'Derek Martinus would have said to him, "The TARDIS gets stolen at the start, and I think there'll be 40 seconds as they chase it down the road and lose sight of it. We'll then cut to this bit where this spooky guy is on the radio, so I just want a note of alarm – three seconds there." Dudley would go away with a list of these things, then write the music, record it and by then the director would be rehearsing the episode, and he would know if things needed changing – scenes running short or long, or things being cut. If he got to Dudley in time, they might change things before the music was recorded, and if not, the tape of the recording would need to be edited. And then the tapes were played in during the studio recordings of each episode, as these early programmes were mixed live.'[64]

The music recording on 9 May was just four days before the first episode was recorded in studio – which was a week ahead of broadcast. Simpson remembered:

'We had a turnaround problem. I don't know what went wrong with the organisation but it got tighter and tighter [...] Sometimes I would have to sit up all night and have my copyist waiting to write it all out. I'd take it into the studio all wet and they'd play it. It was as tight as that. That was very difficult at times.'

In addition to the licensed pop music played in the Tricolour scenes, 18 separate music cues were recorded and dubbed by Simpson for episode 1 of the story, ranging from 5s to 35s in

---

[64] Ayres, interview with author.

duration and totalling 5m 48s – almost a quarter of the episode. 'I always felt that music was very important to productions that I could see on the television,' he remembered. 'And I thought more music would enhance the programme.'[65]

By the time of *You Only Live Twice*, **James Bond** directors knew to leave space for John Barry's music to add scale and emotion. Indeed, Barry recalled being told by the director of another film, 'Unless I get the right score for this movie, I'm dead. I've left whole areas where the composer has to carry the spirit.'[66]

On **Doctor Who**, Simpson could only accent the drama – though there was space for a romantic theme in episode 2, as we'll see in the next chapter. But if he couldn't match Barry's rich orchestration, he could at least bolster the sound of Firman's eight players, as he did for the first appearance of the Dalek. Simpson's invoice to the BBC, dated 17 July, for a total of 41m of music for the whole story, lists 11 consultations with the director and at the Radiophonic Workshop – the BBC department that made special electronic sounds. Mark Ayres explains:

> 'Generally, composers didn't collaborate with the Radiophonic Workshop. When **Doctor Who** started, obviously there was the theme music. [Composer] Ron Grainer basically handed it over to Delia Derbyshire at the workshop, and she realised it electronically. But then the music for individual stories went back to composers. We think the first composer on **Doctor Who** to work with the

---

[65] Simpson, 'The Doctor's Composer'.
[66] 'John Barry', In Tune Sound of Cinema.

workshop was Richard Rodney Bennett on *The Aztecs* [1964], which had some electronic treatment done by – we think – John Baker. And then there was *The Underwater Menace*.'[67]

Simpson recalled that for this story he approached Brian Hodgson at the workshop:

'and asked him to help me create a special sound so that I could have that [...] underwater sound, globule sounds. It was really fun to do. I used to hear snide remarks from the musicians – "Wait till Dudley's finished with this," you know the sort of thing – because I did actually create music and then add it to it. It gave it a body and a sound that musicians couldn't create.'[68]

'Dudley then did the score for *The Macra Terror*,' says Ayres. 'But that was entirely recorded in the workshop because he wanted an electronic sound and also there was no money for live musicians.'[69]

Just as Simpson used the piccolo and bassoon to match the relative scales of characters in *Planet of Giants*, in *The Evil of the Daleks* he uses Firman and his musicians for most of episode 1, and switches to electronic music for the arrival of the Dalek. That accents the sudden twist from the contemporary to the alien and strange.

But this use of electronic music **was** contemporary. In 1966, at the home of music engineer Peter Zinovieff, Delia Derbyshire and Brian

---

[67] Ayres, interview with author.
[68] Simpson, 'The Doctor's Composer'.
[69] Ayres, interview with author.

Hodgson from the Radiophonic Workshop met with Paul McCartney of the Beatles to discuss a potential collaboration. As Mark Brend argues in his history of electronic music, that meeting is an indication of a huge change in popular music, as artists began to look at integrating electronic sounds into their work[70].

On 7 April 1966 at Abbey Road studios, the Beatles overdubbed tape-loops McCartney had recorded at home on to 'Tomorrow Never Knows'. As Ian MacDonald says, 'the tape-loop – a length of [electronic] tape sound edited to itself to create a perpetually cycling signal – is a staple of sound-effects studios and the noise-art idiom known as musique concrète [...] Pop music, though, had heard nothing like this.'[71]

The Beatles continued to explore electronic sound. For all that 'Being for the Benefit of Mr Kite' was inspired by a Victorian poster, post-production on the song included tape effects. And – as we've seen – this strange fusion, this electronic Victoriana, was released to the public on 1 June 1967, five days after 7.5 million people watched Daleks, accompanied by an electronic score, turn up in a Victorian house.

But the music is only one part of what makes the appearance of the Dalek so unsettling. There's also the role we ourselves play in the story.

---

[70] For more on the meeting and its symbolic significance, see the introduction to Brend, Mark, *The Sound of Tomorrow*.
[71] MacDonald, *Revolution in the Head*, p190.

## Sherlock Holmes Vs the Daleks

At the end of episode 1, Kennedy breaks into the secret room in the antique shop, searching – says the camera script – for money. Instead he stumbles on who it is giving Waterfield his orders. The Dalek exterminates Kennedy, and the closing titles roll.

This is the first example of what became an odd tradition in **Doctor Who**, where an episode that begins with an on-screen title clearly naming the Daleks then ends with the shock reveal of a Dalek as if it's a surprise[72]. Arguably, the convention had been set some years before: many viewers of 'World's End' on 21 November 1964 knew from press coverage that it was the first episode of a new Dalek story (*The Dalek Invasion of Earth*). The Daleks also don't appear until the final scene in episode 1 of *The Power of the Daleks*, though the cliffhanger is not based on the revelation they are there. But why would the people making **Doctor Who** do this – not just once but repeatedly?

In a 1966 book, film directors François Truffaut and Alfred Hitchcock discuss the difference between suspense and surprise. Hitchcock gives an example, imagining their conversation as a scene in a film to illustrate the effect on an audience:

---

[72] We glimpse a Dalek midway through episode 1 of their next story, *Day of the Daleks* (1972) before a full reveal for the cliffhanger. The next four **Doctor Who** stories with 'Daleks' in the title – *Planet of the Daleks* (1973), *Death to the Daleks* (1974), *Genesis of the Daleks* (1975) and *Destiny of the Daleks* (1979) all have the shock reveal at the end of episode 1.

'Let us suppose that there is a bomb underneath this table between us. Nothing happens, and then all of a sudden, "Boom!" There is an explosion. The public is surprised, but prior to this surprise, it has seen an absolutely ordinary scene, of no special consequence. Now, let us take a suspense situation. The bomb is underneath the table and the public knows it, probably because they have seen the anarchist place it there. The public is aware that the bomb is going to explode at one o'clock, and there is a clock in the décor. The public can see that it is a quarter to one. In these conditions this innocuous conversation becomes fascinating because the public is participating in the scene. The audience is longing to warn the characters on the screen: "You shouldn't be talking about such trivial matters. There's a bomb beneath you and it's about to explode!"'[73]

Telling us in the titles at the start of the episode that there's a Dalek coming doesn't ruin the surprise, but makes us active participants as we anticipate its appearance. In 1970, Hitchcock went further, telling the American Film Institute:

'Mystery is an intellectual process – like in a whodunnit – but suspense is essentially an emotional process. Therefore, you can only get the suspense element going by giving the audience information. I daresay you've seen many films which have mysterious goings-on [...] and you're about a

---

[73] The full interviews are in Truffaut, François, *Hitchcock/Truffaut*, but this explanation is discussed in depth in Bordwell, David, and Kristin Thompson, *Film Art: An Introduction*, and at Bordwell, David, 'Hitchcock, Lessing and the Bomb Under the Table'.

third of the way through the film before you realise what it's all about. And to me that's completely wasted footage because there's no emotion to it.'[74]

The Doctor and Jamie are caught up in a mystery: someone has stolen the TARDIS, and as they investigate they discover it wasn't an accident but something more sinister which includes murder. But for most of episode 1, this is a story about some lost property and, as Hitchcock says, the audience watching would have no emotional investment. By telling us the Daleks are involved – and showing us Kennedy watching the Doctor and Jamie, and then showing Waterfield and his antiques – we anticipate the disaster to come. The Doctor and Jamie think they're being clever deducing information from clues such as the book of matches, but we know they're walking headlong into a trap. The cliffhanger is not, then, about revealing the Dalek as a surprise, but showing us exactly what the trap is that our heroes will spring in episode 2 – again, the anticipation of that bringing us back to watch the following week.

So, we can understand the reason events play out as they do in this first episode and a half from the perspective of David Whitaker. Harder to explain is why the Daleks conceive of such a convoluted trap. If they're going to knock the Doctor and Jamie unconscious and then spirit them back in time, why not do that at Gatwick? If the point is that the Dalek time machine is housed in a particular building in London – the antique shop – they could still save a lot of time and effort if Bob Hall simply supplied the full address.

---

[74] 'Alfred Hitchcock: the Difference Between Mystery and Suspense'.

The only explanation, surely, is that the Doctor is being played. The Daleks think that if he's simply given an address he'll be wary, but if he thinks he's been clever in discovering the address he'll walk into the antique shop willingly.

The mechanics of the trap are interesting, too. The Dalek wants the Doctor to find the hidden room – that's where he and Jamie will be knocked out – so Kennedy's body is laid out in the study for the Doctor to find. The Doctor then gets Jamie to measure the corridor outside the study, and the corridor is longer, suggesting a concealed room.

As Alan Barnes notes, this trick seems to have been borrowed from the **Sherlock Holmes** story 'The Adventure of the Norwood Builder' (1903), by Arthur Conan Doyle[75]. In episode 1, Waterfield checks that Kennedy, as instructed, left a book of matches in the warehouse for the Doctor to find. Kennedy says yes – the Doctor 'found the cigarettes and the matches.' The cigarettes, the Doctor concludes, must belong to someone other than Bob Hall because he rolled his own, while the matches bear the name of the Tricolour. This clue leads the Doctor and Jamie to the coffee bar, where Waterfield sends Perry to meet them. (The Doctor also deduces that the owner of the book of matches is left-handed.)

In 'The Adventure of the Red Circle' (1911), Sherlock Holmes is presented with two burnt matches and a cigarette end, it being known that he 'can read great things out of small ones.' He easily spots that the matches were used to light cigarettes not cigars, as

---

[75] Barnes, Alan, 'The Fact of Fiction: Lead into Gold – The Evil of the Daleks'. DWM #342.

half the match would have been consumed. From the cigarette end he deduces something more interesting, which leads him to take up a case. A book of matches also plays a key role in a suspenseful scene in the 1943 film *Sherlock Holmes in Washington*.

There'd been a link between Holmes and **Doctor Who** before there'd been a Doctor – Donald Wilson's concept notes for the BBC's putative science fiction series, written on 29 March 1963, suggest a firm of scientific consultants whose cases would have 'almost a feeling of Sherlock Holmes.'[76] We might argue that there's something of Holmes in the first Doctor, such as in 'The Escape' (*The Daleks* episode 3 (1964)) where he and his companions make a series of logical deductions about their captors and are thus able to get free. But the first Doctor is at his most Holmesian in *The War Machines*, where he's an unofficial and unpaid consultant whose brilliance is quickly evident to, and relied on by, the authorities. Having dealt with the crisis that they found so unfathomable, the Doctor slips quietly away, taking no credit – as so often did Holmes.

This, of course, is part of the new take on the series and its lead character introduced by Innes Lloyd and Gerry Davis. In May 1966, the same month that location filming took place on *The War Machines*, Davis was apparently the author of 'The New Dr Who', a memo outlining the appearance and character of the series' new lead, months before Hartnell had even been told he was leaving. 'A feature of the new Dr Who will be the humour on the lines of the sardonic humour of Sherlock Holmes,' says the document. But the

---

[76] Wilson, Donald, 'Concept Notes for New SF Drama'.

first paragraph on the Doctor's 'manner' could apply equally to Holmes: 'Vital and forceful – his actions are controlled by his superior intellect and experience – whereas at times he is a positive man of action, at other times he deals with the situation like a skilled chess player, reasoning and cunningly planning his moves. He has humour and wit and also an overwhelmingly thunderous rage which frightens his companions and others.'[77]

The first words are telling. 'Vital and forceful,' the new Doctor would actively seek adventures, not join them reluctantly or by accident. At the start of *The War Machines*, the first Doctor arrives in London and immediately sniffs out danger: sensing the alienness of the Post Office Tower, which gives him the same feeling as when Daleks are near and leads him into action[78].

In *The Power of the Daleks* the new Doctor has barely introduced himself to his companions before he adopts the guise of an Earth Examiner, allowing him to play detective, spot clues and interrogate colonists on the planet Vulcan. Throughout the stories that follow, he's continually spotting clues that others overlook, conducting tests and experiments to verify his theories. There are the outlandish disguises, the way he pretends to be on a villain's side just to hear their schemes before turning the tables, and the way he exasperates the authorities who slowly come to realise his genius. The Doctor even wields a magnifying glass in *The Power of*

---

[77] 'The New Dr. Who.' BBC Archive.

[78] *The War Machines* episode 1. If this takes place on or close to the same day as episode 1 of *The Evil of the Daleks*, perhaps it's the Dalek in the antique shop he's sensing.

*the Daleks, The Highlanders, The Faceless Ones* and *The Evil of the Daleks.*

The Daleks must understand this connection, because it doesn't seem likely that the matches are Waterfield's idea. He's from 1866 – 21 years before Holmes first appeared in print. Yes, there were tales of detectives before him, but the matches and the hidden room seem too specifically riffing on Holmes. Knowing the Doctor's psychology, the Daleks – apparently familiar with the works of Conan Doyle – devised this ingenious trap. That it works and they catch the Doctor shows how well they understand him.

But it's the parts of the story set in 1866 that really delve into psychology.

# CHAPTER 2: OUTSIDE CANTERBURY, 2 TO 3 JUNE 1866

'I am a professor of a far wider academy, of which human nature is merely a part.'

[The Doctor][79]

## 20,000 BC

In Whitaker's 4 January 1967 outline[80], the Doctor and Jamie find themselves back in 1880, not 1866. They meet Waterfield's wife Anne, and the Doctor is reunited with his TARDIS. Waterfield – despite having access to time travel himself – gets the Doctor to use the TARDIS to take them all back to 20,000 BC. There they meet and capture a caveman, Og, who they bring back to 1880 so that Waterfield can study him.

Note that this requires the Doctor to be fully in control of his TARDIS – which wasn't generally the case in **Doctor Who** at the time. But perhaps the production team had other ideas, albeit briefly. As this outline was written, scripts were being finalised for *The Underwater Menace*, and at the end of episode 4 of that story – recorded in studio on 28 January – the Doctor sets the controls to take the TARDIS to Mars. He doesn't get there, but in the next story it seems that it's the effect of the Gravitron, not the Doctor's inability to control his ship, that has drawn the TARDIS off course to land on the Moon. As Ben jokes, they're 'not too far out'[81]. The

---

[79] *The Evil of the Daleks* episode 5.
[80] BBC Written Archives Centre T5/2,531/1, 4 January 1967.
[81] *The Moonbase* episode 1.

suggestion is that otherwise the Doctor can control the TARDIS when he wants to.

According to Whitaker's original outline, Og would have escaped from Waterfield at the end of episode 4 and then been recaptured in episode 5, where he would have shared a scene with Anne. There's nothing to tell us what that scene might have involved, but we can make an educated guess about it when we come to discuss the role of women in the broadcast version of the story.

Meanwhile, the outline sees the Daleks transport Jamie to their own planet, Skaro, where he meets the Waterfields' daughter Victoria for the first time. The end of the episode sees Waterfield's experiments on Og being taken over by the Daleks.

In episode 2 of the story as broadcast, Maxtible – who does not appear in the original outline – tells the Doctor that the Daleks are looking for some factor possessed by human beings but absent in Daleks that enables humans to defeat them. From what we can tell from the brief two-page outline, this was in the original version, too. Having established this secret factor by studying Og, the Daleks then transport the Doctor and Og back to 20,000 BC to eradicate it from humanity. It's not clear from the outline whether they travel back using the Doctor's TARDIS or their own time-travel technology, but in the story as broadcast the Daleks want to use the TARDIS to spread the Dalek factor through time.

The original version of the final episode sees battles in 20,000 BC and then on Skaro, reuniting the Doctor with Jamie. It seems likely that, as in the broadcast version, the 'human factor' would have been used on some Daleks who would then have caused a civil war. There is no mention of Waterfield, Anne or Victoria in the three brief sentences outlining the episode, but we're told the story ends in Victorian London, suggesting that at least some of the family make it back home.

Note that home seems to be London, not a house outside Canterbury as in the broadcast version, which means that when Waterfield first brings the Doctor and Jamie back in time, they don't also move in space. We don't see where the Doctor and Jamie materialise in the broadcast episode 2, but presumably it's in the cabinet in Maxtible's laboratory.

That the outline of 4 January is so brief, and not even in complete sentences, suggests it's a summary of a conversation Whitaker had with story editor Gerry Davis, and possibly other members of the production team. We don't have evidence of how this outline was received, or what changes were made before Whitaker was commissioned to write the seven scripts nearly three weeks later on 24 January. As discussed, when Whitaker delivered the script of episode 1 on 8 February there was then a major change of brief and he had to rewrite episodes 1 and 2, now without Ben and Polly.

Were Maxtible, mesmerism and the characters of Ruth, Mollie, Toby and Terrall added at this stage, or were they in the story by 24 January? We don't know, but we can see what they add to the story: they exhibit different aspects of psychology and behaviour which add to the story's exploration of what it means to be human. If these aspects were added after Whitaker's original outline of 4 January, they must have come at least in part from story editor Gerry Davis – or possibly from Peter Bryant, who deputised for Innes Lloyd during the week of 9 January and later replaced Davis as story editor. If so, perhaps we can see something here of the story being moulded to fit the production team's aim to make the series more scientific – especially in the character of Maxtible.

Remember that both Whitaker and the writers of the preceding story were asked to include potential companions. Whitaker's outline of 4 January names his character Victoria – an obvious choice for a Victorian character, but Davis later claimed she was named after his own daughter[82]. Does that suggest that of the two potential companions she was his favourite? Again, it's not hard evidence but there's the tantalising sense of the story editor shaping the individual adventure and the series as a whole.

If Pauline Collins hadn't turned down the chance to make Samantha Briggs the new companion, the character would have been in *The Evil of the Daleks*. Shortly, we'll look at how she might have featured in the story as broadcast, but it's easy to see how she would have been fitted into the original outline – she could simply take the place of Anne Waterfield. Anne doesn't appear in the story as broadcast anyway. At least, not in person.

## The Portrait of a Lady

On prominent display in the sitting room of Maxtible's house is a painted portrait of Waterfield's wife. Mrs Waterfield[83] doesn't appear in the story – we're told she died – but the portrait bears a striking resemblance to her daughter, Victoria. That's because it was based on a photograph of Deborah Watling.

---

[82] Vincent-Rudzki, Jan, and Stephen Payne, 'Interview: Gerry Davis'.
[83] Hereafter referred to for convenience as 'Anne', though she isn't named in the broadcast story.

On 11 April, production assistant Tim Combe sent a memo to Mr H Tosh in the Scenery Block at Television Centre asking for a photographer to attend the 25 April location filming at Grim's Dyke house. A photograph was required of the exterior of the house – one, taken at night, was used in episode 4 – and another was needed of Watling in costume for an artist to paint over or from.

Comparing the painting to the available on-set photographs, the closest likeness is one of Victoria leaning on a stone plinth in the garden at Grim's Dyke, looking up and to the left (her right). The position of the head, eyes and mouth are similar, but the figure in the painting has a different hairstyle, necklace and dress. Her left arm is also positioned across her body concealing her right arm while in the photograph Watling's left arm is at her side and her right hand is raised to her shoulder. Either the painter used just the face from this photograph, or worked from another – now lost – photograph taken at the same time, with Watling in a different pose but her head in much the same position.

According to the BBC's filing system, six photographs were taken at Grim's Dyke on 24 April. These include image 67/T1/794, labelled 'Victoria in Maxtible's garden', and two images labelled as portraits of Victoria. That doesn't necessarily mean that either were the basis of the painting – 'portrait' just means an image of someone, usually focused on the face and expression. If the dates given are correct, the images in the filing system were taken the day before Combe requested that a photographer attend filming, so they may be from a separate session anyway. Also, the photograph of the exterior of the house is not included in this list and only exists now as a tele-snap from the broadcast, so the filing system clearly doesn't include every image taken on location. The production team could have decided not to make the image used for the portrait available for publicity, as it might have drawn attention to the painting and distracted from the story.

A number of other photographs exist of Watling in costume on location. 'I took the [other] black-and-white photos of Deborah in the garden at Grim's Dyke,' says costume designer Alexandra Tynan. 'I've noted that those, like the only colour shots from *The Highlanders*, have been credited to other people.'[84]

Chris Thompson says:

> 'I think we subcontracted doing the painting. Or it might have been the scenic artists who did it. But I didn't think it was very good and I might have done something to it afterwards. A picture like that takes days – it's not something you can just do in an afternoon. So I think it would have been a big bit of the budget as well.'[85]

Given the time, effort and cost involved, what role does the portrait play in the story? As we've seen, it's the only remaining link to Anne Waterfield, the character from the original outline. Now its role seems to be to impress Jamie, who finds the subject 'very lovely' before being told by Ruth that Victoria looks just like her mother. When Jamie then discovers that Victoria is being held prisoner by the Daleks, he's keen to rescue her. He's a brave and heroic character, but the suggestion is that he's motivated to help based on what she looks like. It's not that the plot needs him to recognise Victoria when he finally meets her – in episode 4, a Dalek

---

[84] Tynan, Alexandra, interview with author, 11 July 2016.
[85] Thompson, interview with author.

makes her shout out her name for Jamie to hear, confirming her identity.

Why does the portrait need to be of Anne at all? It would serve exactly the same purpose were we told it was a portrait of Victoria. In fact, why go to the bother of making it a painting? Photography existed in 1866, but perhaps a photograph of Victoria would make Jamie more wary of picking up the trail – it was a photograph in the study of the antique shop that led him to being knocked unconscious and brought back to 1866.

However, a painting of Victoria would present a difficulty, as it needs to show her at the age she is in 1866. Why would Maxtible have a recent painting of Waterfield's teenage daughter hanging in his sitting room? Perhaps we could argue that such a picture – and even the portrait of Anne he **does** have – would serve as a reminder to Waterfield that Victoria's safety depends on him carrying out Maxtible's commands. But it would surely also raise the suspicions of other people in the house – Maxtible's own daughter Ruth might find it a bit odd. So, whether or not this is what David Whitaker intended, we can explain the portrait being of Anne rather than Victoria in the context of the story.

John Peel's novelisation provides another explanation, apparently taken from a scene cut from the script of episode 5[86]. As Alan Barnes explained in 2004, in this scene:

> 'the Doctor remarks upon the fact that Maxtible's house contains a great many of Waterfield's possessions. The

---

[86] Peel, John, *Doctor Who: The Evil of the Daleks* p181.

character Terrall tells him that Waterfield went bankrupt, whereupon Maxtible bought up many of his belongings. The Doctor then suggests that Maxtible himself could have forced Waterfield's bankruptcy – after all, a rich man needs no benefactor, but a bankrupt does.'[87]

This information isn't given to us in the broadcast episode, and it's only the Doctor's guess, but it raises a question: has Maxtible always been a villain, or is he corrupted by the Daleks?

If the former, he's much more like the villains of Victorian literature. A lot of Victorian novels hinge on matters of inheritance, with antagonists who seek to control other people and their possessions. As Soames Forsyte says in the first episode of **The Forsyte Saga**, set in 1879, 'Nothing to do with money is trifling,' and much of what follows in that series is about the way he sees everything in financial terms – paintings are judged on whether their value will increase, and he treats his wives as property.

*Our Mutual Friend* by Charles Dickens, first serialised between 1864 and 1865 – a year before the events of *The Evil of the Daleks* – begins with a corpse dragged from the Thames that is apparently the body of John Harmon, a young man set to inherit a fortune. Among other plot threads, we follow the corrupting influence of the money on those it might then fall to. In *The Woman in White* by Wilkie Collins, first serialised between 1858 and 1860, the wicked Count Fosco manages to have young heiress Laura Glyde mistaken for someone else and locked up in an asylum, all as part of a plan to acquire her fortune. Both novels involve questions of identity – in

---

[87] Barnes, 'The Fact of Fiction', p18.

*Our Mutual Friend*, the kind Mr Boffin acts callously as a way of making Bella Wilfer show her true, unselfish character, which is not a million miles from the Doctor tricking Jamie into rescuing Victoria. But Maxtible being an outwardly respectable pillar of society, and using mesmerism to achieve his greedy ends, is surely most like Count Fosco – which we'll discuss further when we address Maxtible the scientist.

Even if Maxtible bought up Waterfield's possessions, it still seems odd to hang a portrait of the man's late wife so prominently in his own sitting room. As discussed, it might be there to underline to Waterfield that Maxtible now owns him and his family. Alternatively, if it hung there before the once benevolent Maxtible was corrupted by the Daleks, perhaps it was meant to welcome Waterfield and Victoria into the household, showing a considerate side to the man? Or perhaps Maxtible had his own attachment to Anne. When Ruth explains to Jamie who the portrait is of, she doesn't say 'my aunt' or some other relation, as she surely would if they were related. So if there was some strong bond, the obvious suggestion is that Maxtible was in love with Anne – but Waterfield married her. That would give Maxtible a motivation to possess and control Waterfield.

It's only speculation, but in other aspects of Maxtible's past we're on surer ground.

## Maxtible and Irving

On 11 April 1967, Innes Lloyd issued the production team on *The Evil of the Daleks* with a five-page document called 'production points'. The same document, printed on pale blue paper, seems to have been sent to the teams working on other **Doctor Who** stories, for the attention of directors and their PAs. It includes the typical schedule for **Doctor Who** – rehearsals from Tuesday to Friday, recording in studio on Saturday – and gives the budget for each episode as £2,750. It also asks for special attention in casting good actors in supporting roles, and requires a minimum of one star actor per story.

Derek Martinus later recalled that, 'At that time, the programme was beginning to make a big impact and star names were attracted.' He put this down to Patrick Troughton having been given the lead role: 'He lent it an air of respectability.'[88]

Except that things weren't quite so simple. On 3 April, the director sent the script of episode 5 to actor Lee Montague, explaining in his covering note that it would give a sense of Maxtible's character, presumably following a conversation they'd had about the role. Montague's name also appears on an undated, typed casting sheet in the production file for the story, and next to him – so apparently equal first choice for the part – is Roy Dotrice. However, Dotrice's name has been crossed through in pen, suggesting he turned down the role before Montague. Below these two names is Paul Hardwick, as a third choice. There's no record of why all three turned down the part, but that Montague agreed to read a script suggests he wasn't otherwise booked. The three men did not appear in any other **Doctor Who** stories.

Tim Combe remembers:

---

[88] Marson, Richard, 'Martinus & Maloney'. DWM #108.

'I told Derek he was really aiming too high with some people. But I suggested Marius Goring because I knew him. His [later] wife, Prudence Fitzgerald, worked at the BBC [as a director and producer]. I probably bumped into Pru in the BBC bar and asked what Marius was doing.'[89]

Goring was a film star probably best known – in 1967 and now – for roles in *A Matter of Life and Death* (1946) and *The Red Shoes* (1948), both the work of Michael Powell and Emeric Pressburger. He was a regular face on television, too, and a report in *The Guardian* from the time says that his name alone could pack the seats of a theatre[90]. He was also enough of a celebrity to have his birthday listed in *The Times* on 23 May (Goring turned 55 the day he began rehearsals on episode 3 of *The Evil of the Daleks*)[91].

If it wasn't a lucky encounter in the BBC bar, Goring might have been brought to mind by recent appearances as two other 19th-century characters. On 16 April, he could be seen on BBC Two as Lord Lichmere in *The Beetle Hunter*, an episode of the series **Sir Arthur Conan Doyle**[92] based on a story first published in June 1898. Goring also starred in *The Bells*, which ran at the Derby Playhouse from 18 to 29 April to rapturous reviews in national newspapers such as *The Guardian*, *The Telegraph*, and *The Times*, with additional coverage in *The Times* and *The Stage* over the next

[89] Combe, interview with author.

[90] Howe-Wallace, Philip, 'Summoned by Bells'. *The Guardian*, 27 April 1967.

[91] 'Court Circular'. The *Times*, 23 May 1967.

[92] 'Sir Arthur Conan Doyle: The Beetle Hunter', BBC Genome Project.

week[93]. On 8 May, Goring was contracted to appear in **Doctor Who**, eight days before starting rehearsals on his first episode.

Martinus told DWM that he was 'quite nervous' about approaching Goring, who accepted the part even though it meant pulling out of a prior commitment[94]. One inducement for preferring **Doctor Who** was that he was well paid: the production file shows he received a slightly higher fee per episode than star Patrick Troughton. 'If Patrick even knew that, he wouldn't have minded,' says Frazer Hines. 'We all knew Marius was perfect for the part. And he and Patrick were old friends.'[95] Troughton had had a regular role in **The Adventures of the Scarlet Pimpernel**, a 1955 series in which Goring was the star.

But Martinus gave DWM a different reason for Goring taking the role:

> 'He was attracted to the indulgence of the part. He liked to play these great Henry-Irving-style eccentrics, and we sold it to him on the basis that here was the chance to create a

---

[93] Howe-Wallace, 'Summoned by Bells'. Shorter, Eric, 'Spine-Chiller of 1871 Still Good Today'. *The Telegraph*, 28 April 1967. Wardle, Irving, 'Lewis's Spine-Chiller Retains its Force'. *The Times*, 26 April 1967. Billington, Michael, 'Repertory Alive and Kicking'. *The Times*, 6 May 1967.

[94] On 27 May, the day Goring recorded episode 3 of the story, he'd originally been booked to narrate Purcell's semi-opera *King Arthur* at the Queen Elizabeth Hall; his place was taken by Margaretta Scott ('Personal', the *Times*, p18).

[95] Hines, interview with the author.

really rich, bizarre character. He seized on that and really went to town.'[96]

One of the great Victorian actors, Henry Irving had his first notable success in his early 30s in a play by James Albery, *Two Roses*, in 1870-71. While appearing in that production, he discovered *The Bells* – a translation published that year by Leopold Lewis of *Le Juis Polonais* (1867) by Emile Erckmann and Alexandre Chatrian.

Set over Christmas 1833, *The Bells* is about an apparently respectable burgomaster, Mathias, who we learn murdered a man called Koveski 15 years previously and then hid his corpse. As the play goes on, Mathias is increasingly haunted by his secret crime. He keeps hearing the bells of Koveski's sleigh – as do the audience but not other characters in the story.

Staged and directed by Irving and starring him as Mathias, *The Bells* opened at the Lyceum Theatre in London on 25 November 1871 – and the effect was electric. '*The Bells* was written to allow an actor to make a series of dramatic effects of mounting power which, properly played, leave an audience emotionally exhausted,' explained *The Times* in 1967[97]. Overnight, Irving became a sensation and he went on to many more celebrated roles, his name now frequently placed alongside great actors such as Burbage and Garrick. In 1895, Irving was the first actor awarded a knighthood. But he never lost touch with Mathias, playing the part some 800 times, the last just two nights before his death in October 1905[98].

---

[96] Marson, 'Martinus & Maloney'.
[97] 'Whose Theatre Is it?' *The Times*, 29 April 1967.
[98] Mayer, *Henry Irving and the Bells*, p1.

In restaging *The Bells* in 1967 – the centenary of the original French version of the play – Goring, the cast and stage management worked from Irving's own script, annotated in his own hand and provided by Irving's grandson, Laurence. 'Alterations were few,' Goring recalled in 1980. 'The main one concerned the music Laurence had also possessed, but all trace of it was lost.'[99] Goring also read Edward Craig's biography, *Henry Irving* (1930) – but Craig's son, the director and designer Edward Carrick, thought this effort at authenticity only hindered the production. Of the version of *The Bells* staged in London in 1968 he wrote to Goring:

> 'I wish to God you had never read Father's book! In the first act, you were so constrained by his description of the man that you were powerless; in the second, you had less to go upon and were better; in the third, you had nothing but yourself and we took off.'

Goring seems to have agreed with the verdict. He calls the London production a fiasco, and in introducing the publication of Irving's annotated script of *The Bells* advises actors to 'read this book; digest every detail; but do not copy what you admire – use it.'[100]

*The Stage* agreed on 4 May that the success of Goring's production in Derby was the result of it being 'no impersonation of Irving [...] but a highly individual performance that has won widespread praise.'[101] An anonymous leader in *The Times* suggested that

---

[99] Goring, 'Foreword', ppxiv-xv. A copy of the score was subsequently discovered.

[100] Goring, 'Foreword', pxvi.

[101] Caption to a photograph of Goring. *The Stage and Television Today*, 4 May 1967, p7.

'Hamlet is Hamlet and Macbeth is Macbeth, but the Mathias of *The Bells* is what an actor makes of him, a blue print, psychologically true so far as it goes, for an actor to make into a personality.'[102]

The success of the play, then, was not down to Goring slavishly recreating Irving's version – an authentically Victorian manner of performance. Instead, it came from approaching this 19th-century character with a contemporary sense of psychology to make Mathias convincing, and affecting, to the audience. In the rather withering view of *The Times*, by playing the role straight and realistically, Goring lifted the material from mere shlock melodrama into something worthy[103].

We can see how he might have applied the same principles to the role of Maxtible in **Doctor Who**. Here, too, a dark secret threatens the veneer of respectability the character presents to those in his household. Here, too, we witness his gradual descent: when we first meet Maxtible in episode 2, he rather cheerfully explains how his scientific interests led him to meet the Daleks; that cheeriness fades as the story progresses and he becomes more obsessed by his Faustian pact; by the end he's lost his home, family and even his humanity, and is apparently last glimpsed, wild eyed and Dalekised, wandering away into the smoke on an alien world. As we've seen, Martinus thought Goring made Maxtible a rich, bizarre character, but the key thing is that over the six episodes in which he appears he is **increasingly** rich and bizarre.

---

[102] Anon, 'Whose Theatre Is it?', p11.
[103] Wardle, 'Lewis's Spine-Chiller Retains its Force'.

Goring clearly embellished David Whitaker's dialogue. It's nothing huge, but in his first scene, for example, Goring twice adds the word 'pray' to his dialogue: 'Please don't get up' in the script becomes 'Pray don't get up', while 'Come with us with and we'll show you how it all began,' becomes 'Pray come with us...'[104] These aren't slips of the tongue, they're a conscious choice to make the dialogue richer and more affected.

But is that an authentically Victorian way of speaking, or just playing to what Goring and the 1960s audience thought sounded suitably old-fashioned? On 20 May, the day Goring recorded this, his first episode of **Doctor Who**, the novelist John Fowles faced the same concern as he wrote *The French Lieutenant's Woman*. As Fowles confided to his diary, he was also:

> '...reading Mrs Gaskell's *Mary Barton* [1848] at the same time. Her dialogue is much more "modern" than mine – full of contractions, and so on. Yet in order for me to convey the century that has passed since the time of my book I am right to invent dialogue much more formal than the Victorians actually spoke. This gives the illusion.'[105]

That distinction between the illusion of history and the authentic past is important when we consider the setting in which this part of the story takes place.

---

[104] Episode 2.
[105] Fowles, *The Journals: Volume 2*, pp27-8.

## Maxtible's House

Before Chris Thompson joined the BBC design department in 1963, he'd been at the Royal College of Art – but being unable to get on to the film and television course there, he studied interior design, much of it contemporary:

> 'Having been at the Royal College, I wasn't that interested in Victoriana. So I had to do research [for *The Evil of the Daleks*]. But the library we had in the BBC design department was really good. Also there was chap in the department, Jim Carter, who was in his mid-60s – almost a Victorian himself. He'd been the designer on all these classic silent movies, and he was absolutely amazing. I'd go to him and say, "How do I do this?" And he had it all stored away in his brain. He'd do these drawings without referring to anything and say, "That's how it should be." He was a fantastic source of information, and a real inspiration for me.'

The studio sets also had to match Grim's Dyke, the house in Harrow Weald just west of London seen in location filming in episodes 3, 4 and 5. 'It was all really high Gothic, wasn't it?', Thompson remembers. 'It looked like Dracula's castle. It was really creepy.'[106] Grim's Dyke was built between 1870 and 1872, designed by architect Norman Shaw for the painter Frederick Goodall. Shaw had already made his name pioneering a particular style of old English house with a Gothic influence – evident in Grim's Dyke, especially the distinctive Gothic arches that can be seen in the tele-snaps.

---

[106] Thompson, interview with author.

The house was a popular filming location. Kevin Brownlow and Andrew Mollo used it in their war film *It Happened Here* (1965)[107]. It appeared in the pilot colour episode of the adventure series **The Saint**, *The Russian Prisoner* (1966), and the same series returned to the house for *The Fiction Makers* (1968)[108]. A month after **Doctor Who** filmed at Grim's Dyke, **The Champions** used the house as a location in *The Mission* (1969), the first of four episodes filmed there[109]. It was used in the horror films *The Blood Beast Terror*, *The Devil Rides Out*, *The Curse of the Crimson Altar* (all 1968) and *Cry of the Banshee* (1970), the comedy *Futtocks End* (1970), the murder mystery *Endless Night* (1972), and the Academy-Award-winning drama *The Prime of Miss Jean Brodie* (1969). **The Avengers**, **Randall and Hopkirk (Deceased)**, **Journey to the Unknown**, **Department S**, **The Adventurer** and **Thriller** also filmed at Grim's Dyke[110].

These productions almost all use the house in a very different way to **Doctor Who**. They are mostly set in the present[111], and usually, the house has been dressed and lit to appear at its best. Looking carefully we can see damage and wear: it conveys faded grandeur, suggesting decay and decadence in the horror films, and in both

---

[107] 'FILM: It Happened Here'. Reel Streets.

[108] Pixley, Andrew, *The Saint: Original Soundtrack Notes*, p6.

[109] Richardson, Michael, *The Champions: Programme Notes*.

[110] Richardson, Michael, *Bowler Hats and Kinky Boots*, p660. Richardson, Michael, *Department S: Programme Notes*, Network Distribution, 2008.

[111] Although *Cry of the Banshee* is set in Elizabethan England, *The Blood Beast Terror* in the 19th century, *The Devil Rides Out* in the 1920s and *The Prime of Miss Jean Brodie* in the 1930s.

*The Prime of Miss Jean Brodie* and *Futtocks End* that the past – its bricks and its values – struggles to survive in the modern world.

Alexandra Tynan remembers the house as 'cold, scruffy and damp, with original Victorian wallpaper peeling off the walls'[112]. That's evident in some of the tele-snaps, and Thompson, who sketched and photographed details of the house so that he could match them in his design for the studio sets, agrees: 'Oh, it was in a really bad state. I seem to remember some sort of toxic thing there, too – it might have been asbestos. There were places we weren't allowed to go because it was dangerous.'[113]

While the first episode and a half of *The Evil of the Daleks* have genuine antiques that are nevertheless brand new, the opposite is true of the house. As it appears in the story, it is old and decayed, but – given that events are set in 1866 – it ought to be brand new. It's as if the house has been corrupted.

For Martinus, Grim's Dyke seems to have been a key ingredient in the success of *The Evil of the Daleks*. Asked in 1986 to choose his favourite of the six **Doctor Who** stories he directed, he said, 'I seem to remember a lot of filming in an old house for *Evil*, which was very good – and the cast were a joy.'[114]

**Doctor Who** began filming at Grim's Dyke on 20 April. This was also Deborah Watling's first day on **Doctor Who**. She later recalled:

---

[112] Tynan, interview with author.
[113] Thompson, interview with author.
[114] Marson, 'Martinus & Maloney'.

'I was nervous, as one always is on such occasions. The first shot was a long corridor with a Dalek marching me down to my cell and it looked quite funny because you couldn't see either of our feet; I glided along and the line of my skirt mirrored that of the Dalek skirts.'[115]

There's nothing in the script about this mirroring of skirts, but it wasn't a new idea. Working on the very first Dalek story, *The Daleks* (1963-64), designer Ray Cusick sought clarification from writer Terry Nation over the description of the creatures in the script as 'legless, moving on a round base'. In 2011, Cusick recalled that Nation mentioned a show he'd seen in London by the Georgia State Dancers:

'I'd seen it too. Terry said: "Do you remember the peasant dance when the girls come on in long dresses and they seem to glide around like they're on roller skates? That's how I think the Daleks should move.'[116]

Tynan can't recall if she was asked to provide a dress for Victoria that matched the shape of the Daleks, or whether the shot juxtaposing the two was the result of the costume she found. 'As *Evil* was in black and white,' she says, 'it was only essential to get the tonal values to read well.'[117]

The off-air photographs don't show the juxtaposition of Victoria's dress with the Daleks, but they do show Martinus using Grim's

---

[115] Watling, *Daddy's Girl*, p48.
[116] Tribe, Steve, and James Goss, *Doctor Who: The Dalek Handbook*, p19.
[117] Tynan, interview with author.

Dyke to full effect, with a shot looking down on Victoria and the Daleks as they pass through one of the distinctive Gothic arches. He remembered that the Daleks:

> 'had to be shot very carefully and from exactly the right angle , because if you shoot them without care they do look rather tame and ordinary. You had to build up a Dalek's entrance. I used to make them lurk in the shadows.'[118]

Some 20 years after the story was broadcast, the effect still haunted fan William Silver, whose memories of the story were included in DWM's 'Nostalgia' feature:

> 'One major asset was its unconventional setting of a stately Victorian mansion, with scenes of Daleks gliding out of wardrobes, through ornate hallways and smashing into fireplaces. I found all this fascinating and strange, but by far the most incongruous sight was yet to come [...] friendly Daleks playing games, ring 'o' ring 'o' roses, spinning round and round chanting "Dizzy, Dizzy, Daleks" and giving the Doctor a ride on their backs.'[119]

That's also why Steven Moffat, the head writer and executive producer of **Doctor Who** from 2010 to 2017, chose the story as a favourite:

> 'One of the great breakthroughs in **Doctor Who** has always been juxtaposition, the odd idea of taking a futuristic thing

---

[118] Marson, 'Martinus & Maloney'.
[119] Cited in Mulkern, Patrick, 'Nostalgia: The Evil of the Daleks'. DWM #128.

and putting it in an old-fashioned setting or the other way round [...] So *Evil of the Daleks* just by virtue of you got to see a Dalek in a Victorian house [...] Yeah, that's just brilliant. It just looked amazing [...] So it's a definite favourite of mine.'[120]

David Whitaker had played a similar trick in his previous story, *The Power of the Daleks* – although set in the future, it features the incongruous sight of Daleks offering to be people's servants. *The Chase* (1965) also put the Daleks in Gothic surroundings, battling a robot Frankenstein's monster and Dracula in a haunted house attraction, while *The Dalek Invasion of Earth* (1964) put the Daleks alongside familiar London landmarks.

Toby Whithouse, writer of several **Doctor Who** stories since 2006, says:

'What's so clever about that is the iconic images, the Daleks on Westminster Bridge, in front of the Houses of Parliament. It reminds me of those pictures of Hitler standing in front of the Eiffel Tower – that chilling mixture of the utterly malevolent with the utterly familiar: places we recognise, that we've been to.'[121]

But it's not just the juxtaposition of the Daleks and Maxtible's house. There are also all the people living there.

---

[120] Moffat, Steven, 'Steven Moffat on The Evil of the Daleks'.
[121] Quoted in Guerrier, Simon, 'Secret Armies', p93.

## Maxtible's Household

The first person the Doctor meets on waking in 1866 is the servant Mollie Dawson, played by Jo Rowbottom. As we saw in the last chapter, Rowbottom had worked for Derek Martinus on stage in 1962. A former BBC secretary, she'd 'dared' – she said in an interview – to audition for the London Academy of Music and Dramatic Art and become an actor[122]. On 25 April 1965, Rowbottom played the title role in *Liza of Lambeth* for the BBC, set in the slums of London at the end of the 19th century. According to a review in *The Stage*, she was 'very pretty and lively and makes a good heroine [...] The period clothes suit her.'[123] Perhaps it was this Martinus had in mind when he considered Rowbottom – not as Mollie but for the Doctor's new companion.

As we've seen, before Rowbottom and Watling were seen for the part of Victoria, Denise Buckley had been offered it, but as a one-off character for this particular story. It's odd to imagine this version of the story, one without Watling – but it might not have featured Rowbottom either.

Alan Barnes argues, persuasively, that had Pauline Collins accepted the offer of her character, Samantha Briggs, joining the TARDIS, she would largely have taken Mollie's role in this story:

> 'Sam would have been the one wondering if Maxtible's house is haunted, helping Jamie to break into the south wing, coming into conflict with the possessed Terrall [...] and

[122] 'Jo, the Girl Who "Dared", Plays Liza'. *The Stage*, 22 April 1965.
[123] Edmund, Bill, 'Liza as a Good, Lusty Fast-Moving Musical'. *The Stage*, 29 April 1965.

ultimately being mesmerised by Maxtible into thinking nothing's wrong. Indeed, isn't it entirely feasible that Mollie Dawson (a character nowhere in Whitaker's original breakdown) could have been expressly created for this very purpose, as a proxy for Samantha Briggs? We note that in her earliest incarnation, Sam went by the name of "Mary Dawson".'[124]

On the DVD commentary of episode 2, Watling says that producer Innes Lloyd told her Victoria's character would be like Alice from Lewis Carroll's *Alice's Adventures in Wonderland* (1865). Carroll himself described Alice as 'loving and gentle', 'courteous', 'trustful' and 'wildly curious [...] with [an] eager enjoyment of Life'[125]. She's also about seven years old in his story.

But Lloyd was probably thinking less of the book than of Watling's performance in the title role of *Alice*, an episode of **The Wednesday Play** written by Dennis Potter and broadcast on 13 October 1965 to mark the 100th anniversary of the book's publication – Watling even appeared on the cover of *Radio Times* to promote the broadcast. Potter's play explores Lewis Carroll's relationship with the real Alice Liddell on whom he based the stories, but she's a very different character. For one thing, Watling was 17 when she played the part, and her Alice is flirtatious and encouraging of Carroll, and then bored by him and condescending.

---

[124] Barnes, 'The Fact of Fiction'.
[125] Cited in Carroll, Lewis, ed Martin Gardner, *The Annotated Alice*, pp25-6.

'Innes Lloyd saw me in that and thought, "Yes, that could be Victoria",' Watling remembered in 1994[126]. She said she didn't audition for the part of Victoria, just went for a meeting with Lloyd, suggesting he already thought she fit the role. But there's little sign of Potter's Alice in *The Evil of the Daleks* – or any of Victoria's subsequent stories. Whereas Polly, Samantha Briggs and Mollie Dawson are rather plucky, bold characters, Victoria is innocent and timid, often someone to whom things happen rather than having the agency to affect the plot of a story herself. Her acts of defiance are limited to protesting at her treatment and feeding her rations to the birds.

There's not a great deal to her – as Watling admitted. 'I was only told that she was a Victorian girl wearing a Victorian dress,' she said in 1984, 'and that her attitudes were to be correspondingly conservative. It was largely left up to me, in other words.'[127]

Archive interviews with Lloyd, story editors Gerry Davis and Peter Bryant, writer David Whitaker and director Derek Martinus offer little insight into their thinking about the character of Victoria, and it's tempting to see that absence as revealing in itself. But the story's incidental music – composed by Dudley Simpson in consultation with Martinus – is perhaps instructive. Simpson recalled:

> 'I remember having to write the music to establish her [first] appearance. And it was completely different to any other

---

[126] Walker, Jane, 'Leatherlungs is Back'. DWM #212.
[127] Marson, Richard, 'Deborah Watling Interview: Archetypal Heroine'. DWM #124.

music I'd written at that stage [for **Doctor Who**]. It had a little romance to it. And I brought the oboe in – it seemed to work beautifully. And then of course [...] when she swings around and spots the Dalek, that's a big contrast. But that I wrote only through being told that there was going to be a picture of her [...] I didn't get a viewing [of the episode] at all.'[128]

This melodic theme bridges the transition between our first close view of the portrait of Anne and our first sight of Victoria. Was that transition originally planned to match up the two faces? As it is, a close up of the head and shoulders of the portrait, gazing up and towards the left of frame, mixes to a closer, head-only shot of Victoria, facing the other way. Simpson's romantic theme plays as she feeds the (heard but not seen) birds through the barred window of the room in which the Daleks keep her prisoner. It underscores her kindness and, as Simpson says, contrasts her with the cruel and alien Daleks, again scored with radiophonic sound. But note that Simpson refers to the 'romance' of Victoria's theme.

As a classically trained musician, Simpson would be familiar with the Romantic movement in music that flourished in the late 18th and early 19th centuries, as typified by composers such as Beethoven and Chopin, where larger orchestras enabled especially lush, rich and emotional music. This was tied to the Romantic movement in the visual arts which, partly in reaction to the Industrial Revolution and the Enlightenment, emphasised the emotional, individual and natural. Another key feature is the

---

[128] Simpson, 'The Doctor's Composer'.

domestic, with a sentimental view of women as nurturing home-makers and peace-makers.

There's something of this in *The Evil of the Daleks*. Women don't drive the plot. In the first episode and a half, set in 1966, the only women to appear are the non-speaking extras in mini-skirts seen in the Tricolour. In the Victorian part of the story, Ruth and Victoria have no more power to change events in the house than Mollie the domestic servant. They can ask questions of the men and encourage them to take action, and in episode 6 Mollie and Ruth promise to look after Terrall – but they react rather than take action themselves. In episode 5, Mollie almost gets to change things, before Maxtible mesmerises her into submission. In the last part of the story, Victoria is the only female character on Skaro, but her actions don't direct or change the plot.

This passivity contrasts with the powerful Daleks, actively hell bent on the conquest of time, but also with the male characters. All the men in the guest cast are active participants in the plot, and none are quite what they appear when we first meet them. We've already discussed Maxtible's transformation in the story, as the veneer he presents to his household comes apart. Waterfield is a well-meaning gentleman forced into a life of crime. Kemel switches sides. Terrall is a good man conditioned to do wrong against his will. Toby – like Kennedy 100 years after him – dies because he's too greedy and tries to steal from his employer, so neither are simply paid henchmen. Bob Hall is in on the scam to steal the TARDIS and dupe the Doctor, and Perry knows the antique shop operates some 'dicey' business, but only calls in the police when Kennedy is murdered. They're still stock archetypes, but they've more dimensions than the women characters.

The Doctor distils the human factor by watching Jamie and Kemel, but given the other characters in the story, it's clear they're not typical men. We're offered a wide range of human characteristics through the story, but they're not all good for battling Daleks. The Doctor admits as much, saying he's captured 'the better part' of humanity: 'Courage, pity, chivalry, friendship, even compassion. Some of the virtues.'[129] He's not included greed or betrayal, even when Kemel switching sides to help Jamie is a good thing.

If the Doctor studied Ruth, Mollie and Victoria instead of Jamie and Kemel, what aspects of the human factor might he have isolated? There's Mollie's courage in daring to help Jamie and to question her master. There's Victoria pitying the birds even when she's held prisoner. There's Ruth's good manners as a hostess, and the way she and Mollie quickly offer friendship to Jamie and the Doctor. They're all compassionate characters, typifying exactly the virtues that the Doctor distils as the best of humanity and uses to battle the Daleks. It's a shame that couldn't have been made more of: that it's not 'male' aggression and deceitfulness that will defeat the Daleks, but 'womanly' soft skills like kindness. It would at least have given the women a more active role in the story.

But that might have been the intention in Whitaker's original outline. There, Waterfield studies the caveman Og to isolate the human factor. Og has to be captured – twice – so is evidently not a willing subject. Then, in episode 5, there's a scene between Anne and Og. What was meant to happen in that scene isn't described in the outline, but it must have been of some importance because it's

---

[129] Episode 5.

included in the 18-word précis of the episode, which ends with the Daleks taking over the study of Og and – at the start of the next episode – learning humanity's secret.

Surely Anne's scene with Og must have offered some insight into the elusive human factor that Waterfield and the Daleks had so far been unable to spot. If it's key to the episode, it must have included some unexpected story beat or twist. The obvious option is for Anne to make some connection with Og, showing compassion, calming him, making a link between humanity in the present and the past. And not by force, the method of Waterfield and the Daleks, but by nurturing him.

Anne and Og do not appear in the broadcast story, but there are echoes of Anne's role in Victoria feeding the birds, and Ruth and Mollie looking after Terrall. It's a rather old-fashioned view of a women's role: nurturing, peace-making, in a domestic space. To an audience watching in 1967, it would probably have seemed Victorian.

'The 19th century is remembered as a time when women's lives were more severely policed and circumscribed than in other historical epochs,' proposes the historian Matthew Sweet – before unpicking that myth:

> 'If this was so, it begs the question why the 19th century was the era in which women first found their political voices, penetrated male-dominated professions, won property rights and carved out their own spheres of professional competence in high-tech jobs that were wholly unrelated to their traditional domestic and sexual roles. Might the widespread presence within Victorian culture of a scepticism

towards and mistrust of male power not explain the preponderance of heavy stepfathers, vicious schoolmasters and weak, deceitful men in its fiction, theatre and art? Who, do we imagine, of the original readership of *Hard Times*, cheered for Mr Gradgrind?'[130]

We can see this in the Victorian novels already referred to. Bella Wilfer in *Our Mutual Friend* is a complex, rounded character, her mercenary attitude to money changing over the course of the novel. In the same novel, Lizzie Hexam is apparently just the kind of self-sacrificing, nurturing romantic heroine that provides the moral centre of the story, and yet she's also active, for example directing her brother Charley's escape from their impoverished home.

Laura Fairlie in *The Woman in White* is another gentle, sweet heroine but the character we remember is her half-sister Marian Halcombe, a fiercely intelligent and resourceful woman who leads the fight against the wicked Count Fosco despite the power he wields over her when she's in his presence. Collins' next novel, *No Name* (first serialised between 1862 and 1863) features a headstrong young heroine in Magdalen Vanstone, who rushes into danger and potential scandal. Collins's *Heart and Science* (first serialised from 1882 to 1883), involves a wicked scientist with mesmeric powers who we'll compare to Maxtible shortly, but the real villain of that story is Mrs Galilee, an overbearing mother all set to ruin the life of her son's fiancée for financial gain.

So *The Evil of the Daleks* presents an inaccurate, 1960s stereotype of Victorian women, and that's a shame because the reality could

---

[130] Sweet, *Inventing the Victorians*, p177.

be more dynamic and interesting – as we see in later **Doctor Who** stories set in Victorian times that play against the tame stereotype: the warrior Leela and the 1980s tomboy Ace clash directly with the genteel clichés of the period, and Clara the adventuring barmaid and nanny is closer to real Victorian fiction[131]. The 2006 story *Tooth and Claw* even presents Queen Victoria as an active, dynamic figure who shoots a would-be assassin.

If the characterisation of women in the script of *The Evil of the Daleks* is a little mundane, the cast are all very good. Watling, given little more to work with in establishing her character than the crinoline dress, makes the most of the part. Her fear of the Daleks is palpable, contributing a lot of the eerie, unsettling atmosphere. Rowbottom is great as Mollie, just as cheeky and engaging as Samantha Briggs – it's a shame Mollie wasn't considered as a companion. Brigit Forsyth is good as Ruth, years before becoming well known as Thelma in the sitcom **Whatever Happened to the Likely Lads?** (1973-74).

As well as the story's treatment of women, its treatment of race is also telling. All the human characters are white and British except for Kemel – who doesn't speak. Trinidad-born actor Sonny Caldinez was represented by the Oriental Casting Agency. He usually took roles that made use of his impressive size and height. On 15 January 1967, he'd appeared as an Egyptian mummy in an episode of **Sir Arthur Conan Doyle**, and over his career played many monsters and heavies, and a variety of different ethnicities

---

[131] In *The Talons of Weng-Chiang* (1977), *Ghost Light* (1989) and *The Snowmen* (2012) respectively.

including Arabs, Indians and, in *Raiders of the Lost Ark* (1981), a character credited as 'mean Mongolian'.

This wasn't unusual for a non-white actor of the time. The **Doctor Who** story after *The Evil of the Daleks*, *The Tomb of the Cybermen* (1967), features Cypriot-born actor George Pastell as the villain Eric Kleig. In his career, Pastell played villainous Russians, Indians, Egyptians, Italians and more – as if looking generally 'foreign' was itself suspicious. But – despite all the Victorian novels in which foreignness suggests villainy – that's not what happens with Kemel.

Nor is it impossible that a black man could also be a Turk – just as it was possible for Martinus to cast black actor Earl Cameron to play Welsh astronaut Williams in *The Tenth Planet*. In fact, Cameron recalls that William Hartnell objected, saying that a black actor **couldn't** play an astronaut, but he was overruled by Martinus[132]. So we can see such issues were being considered and acted on at the time. But whereas *The Tenth Planet* is rather progressive in the role given to a black actor, that's again not true of Kemel.

Alan Barnes suggests that Kemel was named by David Whitaker after Turkish statesman Mustafa Kemel Ataturk (1881-1938), popularly credited with the founding of modern Turkey in 1923. Of course, in the story itself that can't be the case as Kemel is a grown man in 1866, 15 years before Ataturk's birth. Kemel also wears a fez in the story, an item of clothing so linked to traditional 'Oriental' identity that Ataturk, as part of his modernising reforms, banned it from being worn in Turkey. So Kemel seems to have been

---

[132] Cameron discusses this on the DVD commentary on *The Tenth Planet*.

named after a relatively well known and respected Turk, but that's about as far as the association goes.

'Given that Kemel is presented as a dumb brute,' says Barnes, 'using a familiar part of the much-admired Ataturk's name is arguably somewhat insulting.'[133] To a certain extent, that's true, but Kemel is a noble character – devoted to Victoria, brave and self-sacrificing, and with the moral strength to switch sides from Maxtible to Jamie. In contrast to Waterfield and Maxtible, Kemel is uncorrupted by knowledge and the quest for power. The person he's most like is not Ataturk but Jamie, and it's no wonder they soon become friends. The fact he's mute presumably comes from the fact that he takes Og the caveman's role in the story.

The problem with Kemel is that he's a stereotypical 'noble savage'. The phrase had been around since the 17th century and described usually foreign people who seemed more in tune with nature than the so-called civilised westerner. It was enough of a cliché by 1853 for Charles Dickens to denounce the very idea – he argued that such figures were a 'nuisance' and 'enormous superstition', and that it would be better if everyone were fully educated[134]. Of course, the fact he felt the need to say so suggests the noble savage was a staple of Victorian literature, and part of the same sentimental, Romantic reaction to the Enlightenment we discussed before. So there's a precedent for Kemel in genuine Victorian melodrama.

---

[133] Barnes, 'The Fact of Fiction'.
[134] Dickens, Charles, 'The Noble Savage'.

We could argue that Jamie is **also** a noble savage in these terms – the idea was certainly applied to Highlanders in the 19th century, when a Romantic view of Scottish history gripped some Victorians, notably Queen Victoria herself. He's from 1746, so the Victorian setting is to him the future, and in the previous story he responded in horror to the sight of an aeroplane, 'It's a flying beastie!'[135] He's suspicious of machines, robots and experiments, and while technology is seen to corrupt the men of 1866, Jamie remains pure. This purity – this pre-industrial human factor – is what ultimately defeats the Daleks.

However, the noble savage is generally regarded today as an inherently racist stereotype, linked by film director Spike Lee to the 'happy slave' and 'magical negro', in which a black character's abilities and demeanour are there solely to serve white protagonists[136]. The fact that Kemel is mute doesn't help, his inarticulacy another racist cliché. Phil Collinson, producer of **Doctor Who** between 2005 and 2008, noted this of another strong, silent character in the 1971 story *Terror of the Autons*: 'You would [now] deliberately not cast that man as black,' he said. 'It's a different world.'[137]

Times and sensibilities have changed, but surely the writing and casting could have been more sensitive to the issue. As we've seen, in *The Tenth Planet* Martinus cast – and fought to keep – a black

---

[135] *The Faceless Ones* Episode 1.

[136] Gonzalez, Susan, 'Director Spike Lee Slams "Same Old" Black Stereotypes in Today's Films'

[137] Speaking on 'Life on Earth' (extra on the 2011 DVD of *Terror of the Autons*).

actor as an astronaut. In *The Crusade* (1965), writer David Whitaker offers a rich and complex depiction of Muslim characters such as the Sultan Saladin (though the Middle Eastern characters in the story are generally played by white actors). As with the roles given to women, it could be better. In the next chapter, we'll explore another way the production team might have used Kemel.

## Science and Psychology

In episode 5 of *The Evil of the Daleks*, the Doctor takes the elements of the human factor he observed in Jamie and imprints them on to positronic brains which can then be implanted into the three Dalek test subjects.

That they're specifically 'positronic' brains is interesting. For one thing, in *The Power of the Daleks* – the Daleks' previous story, also written by David Whitaker – the scientist Lesterson assumes, twice, that the Daleks have positronic brains. If he's right, then the Doctor in *Evil* is adding a positronic component to what's already a positronic brain, which is a sensible approach as the addition will be compatible. But Lesterson might be wrong; he also thinks the Daleks are robots which they're not – at least, not quite.

In both stories, a 'positronic brain' is an artificial device. Lesterson thinks it must be the source of a Dalek's ability to answer questions on physics and chemistry; in *Evil* it defines how Daleks behave. But 'positronic' has a more specific meaning outside **Doctor Who**.

The positron is a subatomic particle with an equal mass to the electron but an opposite – positive – charge. In 1928, the physicist Paul Dirac proposed that electrons should have such positively charged counterparts, and that many of the other particles that make up normal matter should also have counterparts of equal mass but opposite charge: in other words, he predicted the existence of antimatter.

We now know that several scientists had observed the positron without fully realising what it was before it was finally 'discovered' by Carl David Anderson on 2 August 1932. His findings were published in the scientific journal *Physical Review* in March 1933[138], which also gave the 'positron' its name, and in 1936 he won the Nobel Prize for Physics in recognition of the achievement. Isaac Asimov gave the robot in his short story 'Liar!' – first published in May 1941 – a positronic brain, apparently because the positron was newly discovered and so sounded more cutting-edge than 'electronic'.

In that story, robot RB-34 or 'Herbie' is investigated by 'robopsychologist' Dr Susan Calvin for telling lies – apparently against its programming. Herbie is telepathic and can see what people are thinking, but also programmed to never injure a human. This causes a paradox, as the robot can see that people will be hurt if they find out what others really think – for example were Calvin to learn that the colleague she is attracted to is not attracted to her. Herbie lies to spare people pain, and so obey its program, but that leads Calvin to an embarrassing encounter with her colleague which seems more painful than having been told the truth to begin with.

In Asimov's subsequent robot stories, all set within the same future, we're told that robots – still with positronic brains – are programmed to obey 'Three Laws of Robotics', which aim to

---

[138] Anderson, Carl David, 'The Positive Electron'.

protect humans and the robot itself. Susan Calvin appeared in many of these stories, and the threads between the stories were further underlined when nine of them, including 'Liar!', were collected in *I, Robot* (1950).

As *The Encyclopedia of Science Fiction* says, 'positronic robots' are among 'the best known in the genre; it is not, however a generally used term of SF terminology, few writers having had the cheek to borrow the idea from its inventor.'[139]

As well as being a science fiction writer, Isaac Asimov was also a scientist: at the time 'Liar!' was published, he was completing an MA in chemistry, and by the time *I, Robot* was published he had a PhD in biochemistry. But that doesn't mean positronic brains are scientifically plausible. When particles of matter and antimatter meet they annihilate each other in an intense burst of radiation. David Langford has argued that, as described by Asimov, the positronic brain would be constantly creating and annihilating positrons, generating radiation that would be dangerous to humans[140].

As a scientist, Asimov would have been well aware of the problem but as a science fiction writer he didn't seem to think it mattered. Speaking in 1975 about the scientific implausibility in another of his works, he argued that:

> 'I had to use a kind of plausible gobbledegook [...] But then you see in science fiction you're allowed to depart from scientific possibility provided you know that you're

---

[139] Nicholls, Peter, and David Langford, 'Positronic robots'.
[140] Langford, David, 'Dangerous Thoughts'.

departing from it and can explain it. The reader will go along with you into the realm of fantasy if you will give him an excuse. But to do it without realising you are going into fantasy is insulting to the intelligent reader.'[141]

Whitaker doesn't explain his reference to positronic brains – in both stories, 'positronic' could be synonymous with 'robotic brain'. By the 1960s, Asimov's stories had proven so influential, at least to readers of science fiction, that Whitaker may have used the term to show his familiarity with the genre and its tropes.

But both Whitaker's Dalek stories, as well as mentioning positronic brains, are about the psychology of the Daleks, just as Dr Calvin in Asimov's stories tries to understand what makes the robots tick – and what that reveals about us as humans.

There are those who criticise Whitaker's writing of – and grasp of – science in these and other stories. In 2004, Alan Barnes seized on Maxtible's explanation in episode 2 that he and Waterfield built their device 'following the new investigations 12 years ago by J Clerk Maxwell into electromagnetism and the experiments by Faraday into static electricity.' As Barnes argues, Maxwell:

> '...would not in fact publish his renowned *Treatise on Electricity and Magnetism* until 1873. 12 years prior to the events of *Evil*, in 1854, Maxwell was concluding his mathematical studies at Edinburgh and Cambridge.'[142]

---

[141] Sy Bourgin, 'Interview with Isaac Asimov'. Asimov is speaking about his novelisation of the film *Fantastic Voyage* (1966).
[142] Barnes, 'The Fact of Fiction'.

Graham Kibble-White castigated this apparent error further in a review of the story in 2016:

> 'I've more fact-checking resources in my hip pocket than Whitaker had at his disposal, so it's easy for me to confirm, but Maxwell's *Treatise on Electricity and Magnetism* wasn't published until seven years **after** this adventure's setting. If you are going to try and blind us with science, get it right. Failing that, do what everyone else does – fluff it along with speed [...] Whitaker's continued fidelity to such rubbish results in more discussion, now of mirrors and electrical charges, all told as if in plot terms, it's highly combustible. While it's supposed to provide the pow to propel this epic creaker over the brow and off down the slope to Skaro, it's indicative of the plot as a whole – a doomed exercise in kite-flying for concepts.'[143]

There are two criticisms here: first of the reference to Maxwell being wrong, and then of the description of Maxtible's own experiment of firing static electricity at 144 mirrors. As Kibble-White says, Whitaker did not have the same resources we enjoy now to fact-check his scripts. But that's doesn't mean he skimped on his research.

In *The Power of the Daleks* we can even identify his sources. In episode 3 of that story, Lesterson tests the Dalek by asking it to explain the first law of thermodynamics. 'When heat is transformed into any other kind of energy or vice versa, the total quantity of

---

[143] Kibble-White, Graham, 'The DWM Review: Missing in Action – The Evil of the Daleks'. DWM #498.

energy remains invariable,' responds the Dalek. 'That is to say, the quantity of heat which disappears is equivalent to the quantity of other kind of energy produced.' The 'That is to say' sounds particularly odd coming from a Dalek and is a useful clue that it's a quotation. We can use the devices in our hip pockets to quickly run an online search for the answer given by the Dalek, and find it word for word in the 1911 edition of the *Encyclopaedia Britannica*[144].

That Maxtible mentions J Clerk Maxwell – and Faraday – in *The Evil of the Daleks* suggests that Whitaker had done at least some cursory research into the science of this story, too. The name Maxtible might even owe a debt to Maxwell. Nothing in Maxtible's dialogue – either in the story as broadcast or the camera scripts – when searched for online brings up a match with a reference book, but that only suggests that Whitaker didn't copy out an entry word for word, or that the book he used has not been put online. We might not be able to find the exact volume Whitaker referred to, but looking for a straightforward explanation of Faraday and Maxwell's work led this author to a description that matches the general thrust of what we're told in the story:

> 'In 1831 the British physicist Michael Faraday (1791-1867) demonstrated that an electric field could be produced from a fluctuating magnetic field. In doing so he raised the question of how electrical and magnetic effects might cross empty space. Faraday himself noted the possibility that such

---

[144] See '19. Joule's Determinations of the Mechanical Equivalent' under 'Heat' in '"Hearing" to "Helmond"', The Project Gutenberg EBook of Encyclopaedia Britannica, 11th Edition, Volume 13, Slice 2.

electromagnetic forces might be like "vibrations upon the surface of disturbed water". Then in 1864 the brilliant Cambridge mathematical physicist James Clerk Maxwell (1831-1879) published a complete theory of electromagnetism: according to this, the oscillatory motion of an electric charge would produce energy in the form of an electromagnetic field radiating from this source as waves travelling at constant velocity, that of the speed of light. Maxwell concluded that light was therefore a form of electromagnetic radiation, and that radiation of shorter and longer wavelengths than light should exist.'[145]

That 1864 paper is Maxwell's *A Dynamical Theory of the Electromagnetic Field*, read at the Royal Society on 8 December 1864 and approved for publication in *Philosophical Transactions of the Royal Society* the following June. The journal was probably not bound until November 1865, but Maxwell would have had copies to distribute himself soon after 16 June – almost exactly 12 months before Maxtible's conversation with the Doctor. So if we can believe that Maxtible has made a small slip, and meant '12 months' instead of '12 years', his explanation fits. The '12 years' appears in the camera script, so the slip is by David Whitaker rather than Marius Goring. Perhaps he got muddled in moving the events back 14 years from the original outline's setting of 1880.

If Maxtible had said '18 months', we might assume he'd been at the Royal Society meeting in December 1864 to hear Maxwell's paper

---

[145] Blackburn, David, and Geoffrey Hollister, eds, *Hutchinson Encyclopedia of Modern Technology*, p73.

read. If he'd said 'six months', we might assume he'd read the paper when published in the journal. If it should have been '12 months', that suggests that he was sent the paper by Maxwell personally – that Maxtible is on friendly terms with him, and perhaps Faraday, too.

But another thought is why he's so keen to share this detail with the Doctor. Maxwell died in 1879, before the theories and equations he'd put forward in 1864 were confirmed experimentally by German physicist Heinrich Hertz in 1886, who generated electromagnetic waves and detected them electrically, measuring wavelengths a million times greater than that of visible light[146]. Maxwell's theoretical work in explaining electromagnetism is one of the great achievements of 19th-century science, and without it the theories of relativity and quantum mechanics, and technologies such as radio, television, electronic computers, lasers and the nuclear bomb would not have been possible in the 20th. Does Maxtible know how important Maxwell's work will be, because – through the Daleks – he has glimpsed the future? His eagerness, his excitement, to explain his work to the Doctor would then be because he sees in him a kindred spirit – a scientist ahead of his time.

Kibble-White's second criticism is of Maxtible's experiment: he and Waterfield 'attempted to refine the image in the mirror and then to project it.'[147] To do so, they fired static electricity into a cabinet

---

[146] Blackburn and Hollister, *Hutchinson Encyclopedia of Modern Technology*, p73.
[147] Episode 2.

containing 144 separate, polished mirrors, each subjected to a positive electrical charge. Is this really so risible?

Admittedly, there doesn't seem to be a scientific link to the number 144, other than it is 12 squared or a gross. Perhaps that it's a square means we immediately imagine the arrangement of the mirrors, but 144 is also traditionally used to refer to great size or scale. In the biblical book of *Revelation*, the walls of New Jerusalem are measured by an angel and found to be 144 cubits high[148] – or just over 630 metres. It's a number to inspire awe.

But the mention of static electricity is surely a callback to the very first Dalek story, when the Doctor and his companions deduce from the fact that the Daleks smell like the dodgem cars at a funfair that they must be powered by some kind of static electricity, and use this knowledge to escape from a cell[149]. Whitaker is simply being consistent with established Dalek lore – a detail not only mentioned in the original TV serial, but also in the film version, *Dr Who and the Daleks*, released in 1965. Perhaps looking up static electricity in a reference book for this story led Whitaker to Faraday and Maxwell. The Doctor's response to the term is telling: we can see that it suggests to him exactly who Maxtible answers to. We're already ahead of the Doctor – we know the Daleks are involved – so the detail is there to raise the suspense.

---

[148] *Revelation* 21:17.

[149] 'The Escape'. The deduction that it's static electricity might be wrong. (See Kukula, Marek, and Simon Guerrier, 'The Science of Doctor Who: What Do Daleks Smell Like?')

Secondly, we can watch this scene on DVD. Imagine explaining to someone from 1866 what that DVD actually is, in words they would understand. We might describe it as a special kind of mirrored surface that, when a special kind of bright light is shone on to it, produces moving images and the voices of the dead – at least in the case of the actors playing the Doctor and Maxtible. The phonautograph – the first device able to record sound – was patented in 1857, so a contemporary of Maxtible wouldn't be entirely baffled by the idea, but it would still seem an eerie and strange contraption rather than something grounded in science.

We don't see much of the inside of Maxtible's cabinet, or get much other description of its workings, but the suggestion seems to be that once the static energy was fired into it, it hit one of the 144 mirrors, bounced off – and hit another mirror. The implication is presumably that it bounced round and round, perhaps ever faster and with increasing charge. At least in conception, it's similar to the modern concept of the optical resonating cavity, a component of modern lasers in which an arrangement of mirrors is used to amplify light of particular wavelengths. And it's not a million miles from the principles behind the Large Hadron Collider, used at the cutting edge of particle and high energy physics today, in which particles are repeatedly accelerated around a circular tunnel until they attain speeds close to that of light.

Of course, Whitaker couldn't, in 1967, have been drawing on 21st-century physics. He may have been influenced by popular conceptions of Victorian (pseudo)science. Maxtible's mirrors evoke the conflation of the eccentric scientist with the 'smoke and mirrors' charlatanry of the fairground magician and the psychic medium, who both use mirrors to amaze and deceive their audiences. The idea of reflecting something back and forth in order to enhance and amplify it, perhaps infinitely, is also linked to the concept of a 'perpetual motion machine' – a mythical device that could generate all the energy it needed in order to run and could therefore go on working for ever without an external power supply.

The construction of such a machine was something of a holy grail for the industrially obsessed Victorians, even though another major branch of 19th-century physics – thermodynamics – conclusively showed that such a device was impossible in practice: the universal tendency for entropy to increase ensures that any closed system will inevitably run down without external power. But this didn't stop some people from trying to come up with ways of circumventing the known laws of nature to build one. The idea of achieving some kind of paradigm-shifting scientific breakthrough by bouncing static electricity back and forth is in line with this kind of Victorian 'crank science', and Whitaker may have been playing with the idea of Maxtible as something of an outsider figure, but one who is nevertheless convinced of his own genius.

What kind of scientist is Maxtible? Given the kind of work he's doing in the story, today we'd probably think of him as a physicist – but that was still a relatively new term in 1866. In the 1830s William Whewell coined both 'scientist' and 'physicist' to better describe those people previously called 'natural philosophers' and 'men of science', but the term took some time to catch on. As Jack Meadows explains in *The Victorian Scientist: The Growth of a Profession* (2004), this was in recognition of a change in scientific study, with increasing professionalism, specialism and reliance on evidence from experiments that could be repeated. According to Meadows, this 'pace of change in the scientific community seems

greatest in the period from the 1850s to the late 1870s,'[150] –
exactly when *The Evil of the Daleks* is set. There were those who
resisted the changes: while Whewell coined many new terms
specifically for the work Faraday was conducting as a 'physicist',
'Faraday claimed that he could not even pronounce the word.'[151]

Much of this change depended on funding. 'The question of money
was one that greatly affected how, or whether, a scientist could
pursue his studies,' says Meadows[152]. As he argues, at the start of
the 19th century, the 'men of science' were largely gentlemen
amateurs, self-funding their investigations as a matter of curiosity.
Faraday was relatively unusual in managing to get paid for his work;
Meadows contrasts him with Charles Darwin, whose revolutionary
work in science was supported by a sizeable inheritance[153]. But the
difference between the two men was also down to the subjects
they explored:

> 'When Darwin did carry out experiments, he used either his
> greenhouse or his garden. The needs of chemists and
> physicists were different: for them, the 19th century saw the
> development of the modern laboratory.'[154]

Faraday was able to use the facilities of the Royal Institution, while
there was no practical education at Edinburgh University at all
when Maxwell was a student there – he gained special permission

---

[150] Meadows, Jack, *The Victorian Scientist: The Growth of a Profession*, p1.
[151] Meadows, *The Victorian Scientist*, p2.
[152] Meadows, *The Victorian Scientist*, p50.
[153] Meadows, *The Victorian Scientist*, p169.
[154] Meadows, *The Victorian Scientist*, p58.

to use the laboratory of his professor, James Forbes. Later, Maxwell was made the first professor of the Cavendish Laboratory – an early scientific institution.

So when Maxtible says he has 'the money to indulge my whims' – meaning his experiments – he's fitting a particular type of scientist, or rather man of science. That might explain the breadth of his interests. As we've seen, his experiments are in firing charges of static electricity in controlled conditions, which is what we'd now think of as physics – but his laboratory is full of liquids bubbling and steaming, which we'd think of as chemistry. He's also motivated by the dream of transmuting metals into gold – what he'd consider alchemy, but we now know is possible through the physical process of nuclear fusion. Maxtible is also an accomplished mesmerist, and his experiments on Terrall suggest an interest in psychology. But being a gentleman amateur, he's not had to specialise. In fact, Benjamin Woolley also links Faraday to mesmerism – on which Faraday 'suspended judgment' in 1838[155] – and suggests he saw electrolysis as the key to alchemy[156], which is a neat match for Maxtible.

However, there's a more mundane explanation for Maxtible's apparent interest in chemistry. The script of episode 2 describes Maxtible's work room quite differently from what's seen on screen:

> 'The room is a mass of curved glass pipes with cables inside, complicated machines, enormous coils and retorts.

---

[155] Woolley, Benjamin, *Ada Lovelace: Bride of Science – Romance, Reason and Byron's Daughter*, pp226-7.
[156] Woolley, *Ada Lovelace*, p307.

'Everything appears to be built around, and wires and cables lead to, a large cabinet with semicircular sides and a dome top, large enough to take four people standing up inside.'[157]

The suggestion is that Whitaker wanted a more flashing, sparking electrical set-up, perhaps in the mould of the famous laboratory set produced by Ken Strickfaden for the films *Frankenstein* (1931) and *The Bride of Frankenstein* (1935) – stories in which electricity again plays a key role in the fictional scientific rationale. Chris Thompson recalls:

'I imagine I would have been able to hire some period Victorian electrical stuff but it would have been really expensive. There would probably only have been real equipment, the sort of thing you get in museums. Or you'd have had to build something from scratch, and we didn't have the time or the money. But with the stuff bubbling away, that was easier. That kind of equipment hasn't changed in 100 years, so you could use it new. I would probably have hired 80% of what you see, and the visual effects team would have brought in 20% themselves with things they already had to hand: all the things to make smoke and bubbles. So it would have been a joint effort between the two departments, which made it more affordable and, because it's bubbling away, it looks better on screen.'

Thompson also had to match the laboratory to the Gothic details he'd taken note of at the Grim's Dyke location. He especially

---

[157] Camera script for episode 2, p28.

remembers Maxtible's cabinet, from which the Daleks emerge: 'It didn't have a floor in it because obviously the Daleks wouldn't get in and out if it did. So it was just the walls and the roof, and it was on casters so that it could be pushed around the set.' Does that mean it would have been seen to dematerialise, just like the TARDIS? 'I don't think so. The casters were to help the scene hands.'[158]

A home laboratory equipped for a breadth of investigations also has a real precedent. Woolley describes Andrew Crosse's 'elaborate electrical, chemical and philosophical adaptation,' of his own home, Fyne Court in Somerset, in the 1830s. The electrical equipment was powered by cables that gathered a static charge from the house's grounds[159] – and we could speculate that we'd see something similar were we ever shown the exterior of Maxtible's house in daylight. In a Gothic touch, Woolley says Crosse had a warning notice saying 'Do not touch' – but written in Latin, which meant a non-scholarly servant received a nasty shock. There's a touch of Maxtible about that.

Perhaps, though, Whitaker was not thinking of real examples of scientists, but those in fiction. Maxtible's work room is 'hallowed ground' and the suggestion is that the rest of the household never dare to visit. That's rather like the home laboratory of Dr Benjulia, villain of Wilkie Collins's novel *Heart and Science*. We're told of Benjulia's laboratory that 'When the place wants cleaning, he does the cleaning with his own hands', and he dismisses a servant for

[158] Thompson, interview with author.
[159] Woolley, *Ada Lovelace*, p313-4.

trying to peek in[160]. Benjulia is six feet six, skinny, beardless and has a dark complexion[161] – not very like Maxtible – but he is also 'the sort of man whom no stranger is careless enough to pass without turning round for a second look.'[162] Rumours persist about what he's up to in the laboratory at his suburban home, which we're told is somewhere between Hendon and Willesden – so nearer to the real Grim's Dyke house than Maxtible's home in Canterbury. 'One report says that he is trying to find a way of turning common metals into gold.'[163] When we finally see inside Benjulia's home, the walls are of bare plaster, and there is scant furniture. The old, dilapidated state of Maxtible's home – at least as seen in the scenes shot on location – suggest a similar lack of concern for domestic comfort.

Benjulia is a former doctor who claims to be a chemist but is really a vivisectionist. He's also a skilled mesmerist – with power over animals as well as people. That's also true of Collins' more famous creation, Count Fosco, villain of *The Woman in White*. In episode 5 of *The Evil of the Daleks*, Victoria tells Jamie that she can't remember how she was captured by the Daleks – she just remembers waking up in the bare room where she was held prisoner. In the next scene, we see what must have happened, as Maxtible mesmerises Mollie to forget all her concerns. Fosco mesmerises a young woman in a similar manner, and seems able just to look at people to control them – his wife, Percival Glyde and

---

[160] Collins, Wilkie, *Heart and Science*, p66.
[161] Collins, *Heart and Science*, p63.
[162] Collins, *Heart and Science*, p64.
[163] Collins, *Heart and Science*, p67.

the heroine Marion Halcombe are all compelled to obey. But in the novel, Fosco's power seems to emanate from his foreignness – as Gabrielle Ceraldi argues, 'in the 19th century, mesmerism was popularly associated with the gypsy,' to which she links Fosco's itinerancy and dark complexion[164]. In Maxtible – an English gentleman with a well-established house and home – the powers come directly from science.

In his preface 'to readers in general' of *Heart and Science*, Collins quotes a letter from Sir Walter Scott to underline the moral point of his novel:

> 'I am no great believer in the extreme degree of improvement to be derived from the advancement of Science; for every study of that nature tends, when pushed to a certain extent, to harden the heart.'[165]

That also seems to be the theme of *The Evil of the Daleks*: Maxtible and Waterfield are corrupted by their scientific endeavours and quest for power, and even the Doctor has his heart hardened in conducting his experiment, to the extent that Jamie isn't sure he knows him any more. The cure for Terrall is to abandon the house and be looked after by Ruth and Mollie. It's exactly the sentimental attitude we discussed before, a Victorian reaction to the Enlightenment.

---

[164] Ceraldi, Gabrielle, 'The Crystal Palace, Imperialism and the "Struggle for Existence": Victorian Evolutionary Discourse in Collins's *The Woman in White*' in Bachman, Maria K, and Don Richard Cox, eds, *Reality's Dark Light: The Sensational Wilkie Collins*, p182.
[165] Quoted in Collins, *Heart and Science*, p2.

But there's also a much more 1960s sensibility wrapped up in this. *The Evil of the Daleks* concludes a run of stories where people are taken over and act out of character. The previous story, *The Faceless Ones*, features Chameleon versions of Jamie and Polly – Jamie so different he loses his Scottish accent. In the story before that, *The Macra Terror*, Ben is conditioned to serve the alien regime. The story before, *The Moonbase*, sees a crew of human scientists infected by a mystery virus that makes them puppets of the Cybermen.

These stories all seem to draw on contemporary fears of 'brainwashing', reports of which emerged from the Korean War (1950-53), with claims that the Maoists used coercive techniques to 'turn' their enemies into zealous supporters of their ideology. 'Brainwashing' seemed to explain why western prisoners of war had aided their captors – or, in the case of 21 prisoners of war, chose not to return to the US. The horrible idea of a loyal soldier forced against his will to commit treason was explored by Richard Condon in his 1959 novel, *The Manchurian Candidate*. That was made into an Academy Award nominated film starring Frank Sinatra in 1962, the same year Anthony Burgess's *A Clockwork Orange* was published, in which a violent young man is subjected to an experimental behaviour modification technique that makes him nauseated at the thought of violence – and on hearing classical music. In brainwashing him, the state has robbed him of something fundamentally human.

In 1963, Dirk Bogarde starred in *The Mind Benders*, which explored what techniques might be used to condition an individual. The novel of *The Man with the Golden Gun* (1964) begins with a brainwashed James Bond trying to shoot M, and the film *The*

*Ipcress File* (1965) sees Michael Caine investigate and undergo a new brainwashing technique. On 29 September 1967, ITV began broadcast of **The Prisoner**, a series all about an unnamed agent resisting efforts to indoctrinate him. A 2016 BBC radio documentary listed many further examples from the period. 'The entire subject is mired in fantasy from start to finish,' concludes Professor Daniel Pick, 'not that this means it's not real in its effects.'[166]

The idea isn't new to the Daleks, either. In *The Dalek Invasion of Earth*, the Daleks robotise people, and one character loses his life in trying to get through to his robotised brother[167]. What's different in *The Evil of the Daleks* is that brainwashing isn't only done by the villains – the Daleks and Maxtible. It is also used by the Doctor.

## The Doctor Factor

*The Evil of the Daleks* is about authenticity of different kinds. For the story to work at all, the production team were required to depict three distinct settings authentically: contemporary London, the mid-19th century and the futuristic planet of the Daleks. It is by making those settings credible that the juxtapositions are effective: Victorians in the present day; Daleks in a Victorian mansion; Victorians (and a Highlander) on an alien world. The juxtapositions resonate with us because they feel wrong.

The brand new, yet genuine, antique in episode 2 is another example of the story questioning authenticity. The story is full of characters who are not what they appear and whose authentic

---

[166] 'Brainwash Culture'. Sunday Feature, BBC Radio 3.
[167] 'The Waking Ally' (*The Dalek Invasion of Earth* episode 4, 1964).

selves must be revealed. And it all hinges on an experiment to determine what makes an authentic human – and, in doing so, what makes an authentic Dalek. When those things are mixed up, and we get humanised Daleks and dalekised humans, the result is war. But surely the story is arguing that humanised Daleks are a good thing, a way to stop their evil – isn't it?

We could argue that the only characters who are what they appear are the women – Victoria, Ruth and Mollie – and Jamie. What makes Jamie special is his mercy and decency, but that is isolated and weaponised to defeat the Daleks. Jamie is appalled by this, and by what the Doctor has done.

At the heart of the story is the authenticity of its central character. The pivotal scene in the story, at the end of episode 5, has Jamie question the Doctor: 'You're just too callous [...] You don't give that much for a living soul except yourself [...] Look, Doctor, just whose side are you on?' After 167 episodes of **Doctor Who**, you'd think we'd know who the Doctor is and what he does, but no.

The characterisation of Troughton's Doctor had been much debated when Whitaker wrote his debut in *The Power of the Daleks*, with recording delayed a week to allow extensive rewrites. In May 1967, as *The Evil of the Daleks* was being recorded, producer Innes Lloyd reflected on how that character had changed in the intervening months:

> 'The comedy was intentionally over-emphasised to begin with so that it should be quite clear to the children watching

that this Dr Who was not meant to be the same one, but there's been a levelling off since then.'[168]

It's more than a 'levelling off', it's a conscious shift in tone. The character had been refined since his first appearance – losing his strange-looking hat, his recorder and the penchant for dressing up. But in this scene with Jamie, the character is being shifted in the writing.

Perhaps that's down to new story editor Peter Bryant, who would oversee a darker set of **Doctor Who** stories in the next year. Or it's to raise the stakes before the brutal civil war as the Doctor and his friends find themselves on Skaro.

---

[168] Bilbow, Marjorie, 'Dr Who and a succession of delightful monsters'. *The Stage*, 18 May 1967.

# CHAPTER 3: SKARO (DATE UNKNOWN)

'Without knowing, you have shown the Daleks what their own strength is.'

[The Emperor Dalek][169]

## Death to the Daleks

When David Whitaker was originally briefed by the production team for the story that would become *The Evil of the Daleks*, he was asked to write out companions Ben and Polly, and to write in a potential new companion. But the starting point for his story was a third requirement: to kill off the Daleks.

The Daleks were – and remain – a key part of **Doctor Who**. Their first appearance, in the second **Doctor Who** story, helped establish the series, and their subsequent stories saw peaks in the numbers of people watching. When the production team took the risky step of recasting **Doctor Who**'s lead actor in 1966, they cushioned the blow by having this new incarnation immediately face *The Power of the Daleks*. Viewers stuck with the programme.

The Daleks were also a cultural phenomenon. There was a huge volume of licensed, Dalek-related merchandise available to buy – Louis Marx & Company sold half a million battery-operated toy Daleks in 1965, and the royalties to the BBC of this single line of toys produced by just one of the many Dalek licensees were some £4,500 – more than the budget for two episodes of **Doctor Who** at

---

[169] Episode 6.

the time[170]. Their influence extended far beyond that. Daleks were easy to mimic and instantly recognisable, ideal for children to play and draw. But what the Daleks represented – their cold logic and ruthless inhumanity – meant they were also used to make points in political cartoons in newspapers. A month before the broadcast of *The Power of the Daleks*, a future MP and member of the House of Lords, Hugh Dykes, was at the Conservative Party conference, where he accused Defence Secretary Denis Healey of being 'the Dalek of defence, pointing a metal finger at the armed forces and saying, "We will eliminate you."' As Alwyn Turner says, Dykes got the Daleks' catchphrase wrong – and they don't have fingers, either – but 'it was nonetheless a sign of how readily the creatures had passed into the language.'[171]

Given this extraordinary impact, why was *The Evil of the Daleks* intended to be their final appearance? In part, it was because of their enormous success.

Writer Terry Nation effectively co-owned the Daleks with the BBC[172] and received the same share of the royalties from licensing, so his creations quickly made him very wealthy. But it seems the success of his Dalek scripts also led directly to his writing for TV series such as **The Saint** (1962-69) and **The Baron** (1966-67). These were slick, stylish adventure series, shot on film and with much

---

[170] Bentley, 'Your Own Dalek', p44.

[171] *The Guardian*, 15 October 1966, quoted in Alwyn Turner, *Terry Nation: The Man Who Invented the Daleks*, p100.

[172] 'While the concept of the Daleks was owned by the Nation estate, the design was entirely the BBC's' (Rees, Dylan, *Downtime: The Lost Years of Doctor Who*, p182).

higher budgets than **Doctor Who**. They were made for broadcast on ITV, but with the express intention of also being sold to the big television networks in the US. It seems that as part of his work on **The Baron**, Nation regularly flew to the US to meet with these networks.

*The Sun* reported as early as 3 August 1965 that Nation was 'negotiating with TV companies for the rights of what they want to call "The Dalek Show".'[173] In May 1966, Nation and his business partner, the American toy tycoon Fred Alper, met with BBC TV Enterprises – the commercial arm of the BBC – to discuss co-funding a Dalek series. Given the potential returns, BBC TV Enterprises were keen. Nation delivered a pilot script and budget breakdown on 21 October – the day before the studio recording of episode 1 of *The Power of the Daleks*.

The BBC were required to provide half the £40,000 budget and were prepared to do so for a single pilot episode. However, Nation and Alper were keen to begin shooting on 12 December – or earlier – as they wanted the pilot completed in time to show the US networks in March 1967, when the networks would decide on what series to commission for broadcast in the autumn. Even before a contract had been signed with the BBC, Nation's team were booking studio facilities, and were in contact with the production team on **Doctor Who** about hiring the Dalek props once *The Power of the Daleks* completed recording. But the BBC baulked at signing

---

[173] Pixley, 'Daleks: Invasion USA 1967 AD', p19. See the article for more detail on the proposed Dalek series and why it didn't happen.

a commitment to a full series – not just a pilot – if the US networks showed interest.

By 25 November, it was clear to Nation and Alper that the BBC would not sign the contract. Nation and Alper agreed to pay the costs for the now unused studio facilities, but a last-chance bid was also made to save the project by getting BBC Two to commit to broadcasting 'The Daleks' if it was taken up by US networks. However, on 23 December, David Attenborough – the controller of BBC Two – confirmed, regretfully, that he could not 'place such a series.'[174]

That date might have a bearing on what happened next. After all, there seems no reason why, if the BBC had been involved in making a Dalek series, the Daleks couldn't also continue to appear in **Doctor Who**. Some kind of cross-over might have helped establish the new series – as with the appearance of the 12th Doctor in the first episode of the 2016 **Doctor Who** spin-off, **Class**.

So it seems likely that *The Evil of the Daleks* was commissioned **after** the BBC backed out of any commitment to the Dalek series, perhaps even after Attenborough's decision of 23 December. On 4 January 1967, David Whitaker supplied a summary outline of his story, apparently following discussions with the production team. The suggestion, then, is that the story was commissioned quickly – because it had to be.

We can glean some sense of the atmosphere between Nation's team and the BBC from what followed. On 26 January – two days

---

[174] Pixley, 'Daleks: Invasion USA', p28.

after Whitaker was commissioned to write the scripts – Nation and his representatives met with BBC TV Enterprises to discuss how he might continue with his efforts to get a Dalek series made. But at that meeting, as reported by Enterprises, 'It became apparent that Terry Nation did not want the BBC to participate in his venture at all.'[175]

It seemed he didn't want the BBC to have any stake in the Daleks. On 2 February, John Henderson, assistant head of copyright at the BBC, wrote to Nation's agent, Beryl Vertue, to confirm what had been agreed in their discussions: the BBC had until 31 December to broadcast a final Dalek story, which it could show only once. The BBC would, confirmed Henderson, endeavour to show it by 30 September – suggesting a contingency to hold back broadcast until after the series' summer break as the opening story of its fifth season, but one that would not hamper a Dalek TV series debuting that autumn, too. On 11 May, Roy Williams, commercial manager at BBC TV Enterprises, wrote to all remaining Dalek licensees to inform them that their licenses would expire when 'the BBC's rights in The Daleks revert to Mr Terry Nation on 31 December 1967.'[176]

Withdrawing the Daleks from the BBC and the licensees would support the potential sale of the Dalek TV series – any network who bought it would then also have exclusive rights to the Daleks and their lucrative merchandising. But one wonders how David Whitaker felt about the potential loss of revenue.

---

[175] Pixley, 'Daleks: Invasion USA', p29.
[176] Bentley, p50.

## Whitaker Vs Nation

In 1964, David Whitaker novelised the first Dalek TV story and also collaborated with Terry Nation on *The Dalek Book*, which sold 75,000 copies[177]. From 23 January 1965, the comic *TV Century 21* ran a single-page, Doctorless Dalek comic strip in each weekly issue – Nation advising on the first story but the 104 instalments that ran until January 1967 otherwise written by Whitaker. Whitaker and Nation collaborated on two further books published that year – *The Dalek World* and *The Dalek Pocketbook and Space Travellers Guide* – and Whitaker also wrote a stage play, *The Curse of the Daleks*, which ran at the Wyndham Theatre from 21 December 1965, apparently at least in some connection with Nation.

The books in particular provide much more detail about the Daleks than anything seen in the TV episodes. For example, *The Dalek Book* includes a cutaway illustration showing the anatomy of a Dalek, a map of the Dalek planet Skaro and a Dalek dictionary. The stories in that book tell of Dalek incursions into the Solar System and the human efforts to battle them – before the events of *The Dalek Invasion of Earth*, broadcast two months after publication. One comic strip in the book, 'City of the Daleks', gives readers a more detailed tour of the Daleks' home than is seen in the first Dalek story – and in full colour, too. The same strip introduces a hierarchy of Daleks, with a red War Leader Dalek co-ordinating Dalek activity, a red Storm-Blast Dalek acting as a sort of 'sergeant major', and the Dalek Emperor, feeding on revitalising rays.

---

[177] 'The Dalek Book (David Whitaker & Terry Nation)' at Doctor Who Toybox.

In his TV **Doctor Who** stories, Nation preferred not to reveal much about his creations. We hear nothing of their language on screen, for example. Something of a hierarchy is seen in *The Dalek Invasion of Earth* – a black Dalek gives orders to the other, grey Daleks and in turn answers to 'Supreme Command' – and slight modifications were made to the Daleks' design and voices in these early years. But generally the Daleks remain as they were in their first story: an army of merciless conquerors, bursting out unexpectedly, grating commands and exterminating anyone who doesn't obey. It's the same when they invade London in the 22nd century as it is when they arrive in a haunted house to battle robots of Frankenstein's monster and Dracula, and again when they turn up in ancient Egypt. They might have new technology with which to threaten the Doctor, or new and gruesome allies, but the Daleks themselves don't develop, at least in the stories written by Nation.

Of course, licensed publications could assume an audience eager for more information about the Daleks, while the TV show was aimed at a broader audience of more casual viewers who just wanted a fast-moving adventure. The details in books and comics might be reread and even pored over, whereas a TV episode was, at the time, unlikely to be seen again. Printed stories could include plenty of Dalek dialogue without it having to be rendered through the ring modulator that produced the grating tones heard on TV, and which Nation admitted got boring if not kept to short bursts[178].

So in the spin-off publications and productions, he and Whitaker – it seems it was largely Whitaker – delved into every aspect of the

---

[178] Rudin, Dave, 'Archive Interview with Terry Nation!'

Dalek culture, the stories often about ordinary civilians being awed by encounters with Daleks and Dalek life. But on TV, Nation focused on rallying people to fight back against this implacable, unchanging force. In the first Dalek story, the Doctor and his companions must convince the other natives of Skaro, the Thals, to stand against the Daleks. In the next story, there's a human resistance against the invasion of Earth. In *The Chase*, the Doctor and his friends are pursued through time and space by the Daleks until they meet another race of machines, the Mechanoids, which prove a match for the Daleks.

Then, in *The Daleks' Master Plan* (1965-66), agents of the Space Security Service must be convinced that it's not the Doctor who threatens the Earth but Mavic Chen – guardian of the Solar System and the very man the agents answer to. Agent Sara Kingdom coldly shoots her own brother, Bret Vyon, for helping the 'fugitive' Doctor, before being convinced of the truth and helping him to stop the Daleks – giving her life to do so in the final episode of the story, 'Destruction of Time'.

Nation clearly saw in Sara the way to spin out Dalek stories independent of the Doctor. He resurrected her in *The Dalek Outer Space Book* – a fourth book of stories and features exploring the Daleks, published on 8 September 1966. Sara was also the star of the pilot script he delivered the following month for the Dalek TV series. As Andrew Pixley says, the book afforded Nation 'the luxury of a dry run' for the concepts and characters in the pilot[179].

---

[179] Pixley, 'Daleks: Invasion USA'.

But while the previous Dalek books had been written with David Whitaker, Whitaker and Nation's last collaboration seems to have been on the stage play *The Curse of the Daleks*, which ran over the winter of 1965-66. Whitaker didn't contribute to *The Dalek Outer Space Book*. Alwyn Turner cites one source claiming that Whitaker and Nation even had a 'terrible fight', Nation unable to 'handle this Oxbridge attitude'[180] – though Whitaker was not Oxbridge educated.

There's little definitive evidence in the archives or other interviews to corroborate the story[181]. That's not to say a fight didn't happen, just that we should be wary of reading too much into a single account of one argument in all the years the two men worked together. But there are reasons they might have quarrelled.

As the original story editor on **Doctor Who**, Whitaker had invited Nation to contribute to the series in the first place. 'Ironically,' Whitaker recalled in the late 1970s, 'he didn't want to write for us, considering it rather demeaning that he had even been asked.'[182]

---

[180] Turner, *Terry Nation*, p146.

[181] Brad Ashton, part author of *The Dalek Outer Space Book,* for instance, has said that 'as far as I know they got along pretty well' (Ashton, Brad, 'A Cheque on the Table', *Vworp Vworp* #3, p98). The same issue of the fanzine *Vworp Vworp* (received as this book was going to press) quotes Paul Fishman, Turner's source for the Whitaker-Nation fight, as saying that Whitaker 'literally made a quick departure as Terry couldn't stand him and one day totally lost it and hit him [...] Whitaker did not return' (Brockhurst, Colin, 'The Ideas Boy', *Vworp Vworp* #3, p97).

[182] Marson, Richard, 'Whitaker's World of Doctor Who', DWM #98.

Nation remembered that he bluntly turned down the offer and then immediately fell out with the man he was working for, comedian Tony Hancock – who fell out with many collaborators over the years, so it's not necessarily a sign of Nation having past form. Nation found himself out of a job and despite having turned down Whitaker's offer went to see him. 'I came up with a story idea,' Nation later said of how the production team took him on. 'Anyway, they liked it, they bought it, and that takes us up to where the Daleks started.'[183]

Except that rather glosses over Whitaker's role in getting the story commissioned and made. First he had to convince producer Verity Lambert, who 'thought it sounded like a good idea.'[184] It was harder to persuade head of serials Donald Wilson and head of drama Sydney Newman – the creators of **Doctor Who**. Newman had famously forbidden Lambert from including bug-eyed monsters in the series. Lambert later recalled:

> 'Donald Wilson hated it. He called David and I in and said he had read the scripts and thought they were terrible. He didn't like the idea, he didn't like the writing... In fact he virtually told us we shouldn't do it.'[185]

Whitaker himself later remembered:

> 'The row came when it was thought that the Daleks would drag the show down to being puerile rubbish. One of our

---

[183] Nazarro, 'Interview'.

[184] Lambert, 'Creation of the Daleks' (extra on the 2006 DVD release of *The Daleks*).

[185] Bentham, Jeremy, *Doctor Who: The Early Years*, p95.

prime intentions was to keep an educational slant to it and Daleks were not felt to be in the right mould at all.'

He and Lambert persisted, and with no other scripts ready in time, Newman had to give way – admitting his error when the Daleks proved such a success. But some 15 years later, Whitaker was still keen to defend his commission:

'Actually, that Dalek story **was** educational, in an especially subtle way – it showed the dangers of war, pacifism and racial hatred. It contained many admirable and idealistic truths in it and it was also a jolly good adventure story.'[186]

Whitaker getting the story commissioned was one thing, then there was the writing. 'Terry did write a good script,' Lambert recalled, 'but David sometimes put a bit of substance into our main characters.'

Director Richard Martin, who worked on the first three Dalek stories, agreed:

'I think David nursed [Nation] along a lot with the dialogue because David was a very thoughtful, very quiet, very intelligent man, who would tend to find the human element in something which would otherwise simply be a wham-bam-thank-you-ma'am-type thriller.'[187]

So without Whitaker there would never have been any Daleks, and their first two stories would have lacked emotional impact. It's no wonder Nation trusted Whitaker to write the novelisation and

---

[186] Marson, 'Whitaker's World of Doctor Who'.

[187] Lambert and Martin, 'Creation of the Daleks'.

other books, the comic strip and stage play, as well as additional dialogue for the second of the Dalek movies.

But these things were making Nation – and Nation alone – very wealthy. Others felt somewhat aggrieved. Raymond Cusick, the designer who played a key role in the look of the Daleks, later remembered:

> 'I was quite friendly then with Terry Nation. We appeared on a very famous show on BBC Two called **Late Night Line-Up**. And I remember asking him after the show, "What about the films, Terry?" And he said, "Leave it to me." And I never saw him again.'[188]

Nation's attitude to this is telling. In 1989, he said that Cusick:

> '...made a tremendous contribution, and I would love to be glib enough to put it into percentage terms, but you can't do that. You start with something that is a writer's dream that he's put down into words, and amended, and added to in conversations.'

In other words, the Daleks belonged to him as the original writer, in no uncertain terms and whatever anyone else might have contributed. 'Cusick didn't get anything,' he admitted, 'but he was a salaried employee, and I think he knew the nature of his work.'[189] That seems to have rankled with Cusick; did it also rankle with Whitaker?

---

[188] Cusick, speaking on 'Daleks – The Early Years'.
[189] Nazarro, 'Interview'.

Brad Ashton, who – like Nation and Whitaker – was represented by the ALS agency, remembered that he was taken on to co-write *The Dalek Outer Space Book* in 1966 because Nation was too ill to complete the job himself, but doesn't recall any difficulties between Nation and Whitaker. The book was one, smallish job in Ashton's long career and he doesn't remember much about what was involved but something that stayed with him is the issue of his fee. 'I do remember being very disappointed that all I got paid for writing two-thirds of the book was £189,' he recalled in an interview with Marcus Hearn in 2016. 'David Whitaker, who had written most of the previous year's edition , told me he was paid £1000.'[190]

Perhaps Whitaker had been offered this reduced fee and turned it down. Or perhaps he felt more generally aggrieved not to share in the financial rewards from something he'd helped to create.

For his 1986 book *Doctor Who: The Early Years*, Jeremy Bentham spoke to June Barry, who was married to Whitaker at the time he worked on **Doctor Who**. She said:

> 'David crafted and shaped **Doctor Who**. Sydney [Newman] and Donald [Wilson] evolved the frame, but the myth came from him. He worked harder on the show than anyone else, steering many of the writers he brought into **Doctor Who**. And he created far more than he is ever given credit for...'[191]

But that's a complaint about Whitaker's role in the early years of **Doctor Who** generally, not about the Daleks in particular. Did Barry

---

[190] Ashton, Brad, 'A Cheque on the Table', p98.
[191] Bentham, *The Early Years*, p70.

say anything else to Bentham, not included in his book, that might suggest any bitterness towards Nation?

> 'Sadly, I don't have any more of my interview with June than was published. [...] I certainly wouldn't describe her as sounding angry or embittered, more straightforward and matter-of-fact in describing the situation as it stood about David's position under the shadows of Nation, Lambert and Newman.'[192]

Bentham's book describes Whitaker falling out with another **Doctor Who** writer – Anthony Coburn, who wrote the first four broadcast episodes and another six-part script that was shelved in favour of Nation's Dalek story. Whitaker does not even mention Coburn in a letter dated 28 October 1978 that he wrote to fan Gary Hopkins about the early days of **Doctor Who**. In describing the 'great restrictions' under which **Doctor Who** was made, he praises designer Ray Cusick, 'fine directors such as Waris Hussein and Douglas Camfield', producer Verity Lambert and the cast. He also singles out four 'fine writers' from that early period: John Lucarroti, Dennis Spooner, Louis Marks and Terry Nation. There's no hint of animosity: the Daleks were, he said, 'worthy of Jules Verne'[193]. He made the same link to the 19th-century writer who had such a profound influence on 20th-century science fiction in his correspondence to fan Guy Deveson, written about the same time.

---

[192] Bentham, Jeremy, interview with author, 19 August 2016.
[193] Gary Hopkins kindly shared a copy of this letter.

'The Daleks were a smashing invention,' he added, 'and I took to them at once.'[194]

June Barry described Whitaker as having 'impeccable manners that somehow always reminded you of an older, bygone age,'[195] so perhaps it should be no surprise that even if there had been a big falling-out between him and Nation he didn't mention it in his letters to fans. But Nation, too, spoke fondly of Whitaker: 'I got along well with David,' he said in 1995. 'He supported me very thoroughly.'[196]

But something might suggest Whitaker felt cheated. Since at least June 1961[197], he'd been a member of what became known as the Writers' Guild of Great Britain. His name appears in the organisation's publications on an infrequent basis – usually mentioning things he was working on, though *The Screenwriter Quarterly* of winter 1962-63 also announced his engagement to June Barry, the space afforded and jokey tone suggesting Whitaker was a well-known figure in the community[198]. But at around the same time as his supposed fight with Nation, he started taking a much more active role in championing the rights of writers. On 8 July 1965, Whitaker asked questions at the Guild's extraordinary

---

[194] Quoted in Marson, 'Whitaker's World of Doctor Who'.

[195] Bentham, *The Early Years*, p60.

[196] Turner, *Terry Nation*, p146.

[197] 'The Coming Quarter: What Some Guild Members Will Be Working On In The Next Three Months'. *Guild News: The Journal of the Television & Screen Writers' Guild*, 5 June 1961.

[198] 'June Wedding for David Whitaker'. *The Screenwriter Quarterly* #11, Winter 1962-63.

general meeting[199], and it seems that in November – just before the opening of *The Curse of the Daleks* stage play, his last collaboration with Nation – he joined the Guild's executive council. A year later on 29 October 1966, the day the second episode of his *The Power of the Daleks* was recorded at Riverside Studio, Whitaker was unanimously voted in as chair of the Writers' Guild – suggesting his work on the board over the preceding months, as well as his experience as a writer and his good manners, had been widely recognised.

With so little hard evidence, it's tempting to wonder if Whitaker was politicised because he felt cheated with respect to the Daleks. If so, we might look for glimpses in *The Evil of the Daleks* – which Whitaker wrote while chair of the Writers' Guild – for clues as to his feelings about the situation with Nation. Maxtible is consumed by greed, making a Faustian pact with the Daleks so that he might learn how to turn lead into gold, and in doing so he exploits the skills of the well-meaning but corrupted Waterfield, whose good manners are from a bygone age...

All right, it's a bit of a stretch – though we'll return to the idea shortly. But whatever the personal differences between Whitaker and Nation, Nation really didn't like Whitaker's Dalek stories for TV.

## Power Vs Pilot

'I didn't like them, and I responded very badly to them,' Nation later said:

---

[199] 'Extraordinary General Meeting: The ITV Royalties Battle; Two New Branches; A New Name, & New Rules'. *Screenwriter* 18 Autumn 1965.

'The Daleks were something that I understood better than anybody else. It appeared [in Whitaker's stories] that they were simple robots, and all you'd have them do was say "Exterminate," and you'd have it made. They were very much more complex in the way they should be presented. I didn't like David's episodes, where he had them being very sweet, and very polite; that seemed totally alien to me. This is not to say that they were not good episodes; this is just my personal opinion.'[200]

Now, this was Nation recalling the stories more than 20 years after he'd seen them, but it still seems a little unfair. In fact, it was Whitaker who offered more depth and complexity to the Daleks while Nation kept them broadly the same from story to story. That's clearly evident in the pilot script he submitted to the BBC on 21 October 1966 – not least because so much of it lifts from his **Doctor Who** episodes from the previous year[201]. Like the pilot, Nation's 1965 **Doctor Who** episode *Mission to the Unknown* involves agents of the Space Security Service being attacked by the vegetation on an alien world before discovering a Dalek plot to attack the Solar System.

When the Daleks are first seen in the pilot, they chant 'Attack and destroy!' before obliterating the dome of Explorer Base One. The Daleks give orders and annihilate people unless they are, and as

---

[200] Nazarro, 'Interview', p21.

[201] Nation's pilot script is not generally available but the author has seen a copy. An audio adaptation produced by Big Finish Productions can be found on *Doctor Who: The Lost Stories – The Second Doctor Box Set*.

soon as they cease being, useful, but otherwise we learn nothing about them. They have concealed a mechanism in a rock face that extends steel bars across a chasm so they can cross it, but that's the extent of their ingenuity.

Sara is, just like in *The Daleks' Master Plan*, tough and apparently unfeeling until something happens to her brother (a different brother this time). Sara's robot companion Mark Seven genuinely lacks emotion and there's no humour in the story to alleviate tension. The only emotions are fear and excitement, the short, snappy dialogue in the script ending in multiple explanation marks. The result is a brutal, thrilling adventure – but a cold one with little depth.

In some ways, the tone of the story is quite like *The Power of the Daleks*, which was in production when Nation delivered his pilot script, and which had been commissioned from Whitaker on 22 July. But in the **Doctor Who** story, the Daleks are a much more devious force, pretending to be the willing servants of human colonists so that they can secretly build up a new army of Daleks. The plot draws on elements of Whitaker's stage play, *The Curse of the Daleks* – perhaps it's no coincidence that Nicholas Hawtrey appeared in both productions. *The Times* felt the play depended too much on 'weak jokes'[202], so there was at least some attempt at levity. In the otherwise grim TV story, the new incarnation of the Doctor and his companions Ben and Polly provide comic relief, but the Doctor's past relationship with the Daleks also adds a layer of depth: he's the only one in the story to know what the Daleks really

---

[202] 'The Daleks Come To Life'. *The Times*, 22 December 1965.

are, while they confirm his identity when even Ben and Polly doubt him. The other characters in the story are variously scheming and not quite what they appear, and though some of this may be the result of adjustments made to Whitaker's scripts by Dennis Spooner, the result is a richer, more complex story than Nation's TV pilot.

Charles Norton, who in 2016 produced an animated version of *The Power of the Daleks*, says:

> 'You can see the story and the Daleks as a whole really benefit from having a new writer. It's a good example of doing something new and intelligent with them. There's only so often you can have Daleks trying to invade a planet before it gets a bit repetitive. David Whitaker made the Daleks not so much more rounded characters but a more interesting force. By scaling the whole thing back to a small group of people and small group of Daleks, enclosing the whole thing and giving the Daleks something to do that's genuinely calculated and beyond simply wanting to invade the planet, you make them more credible and interesting, and frightening. It's probably the strongest Dalek story from the 1960s for that reason.'[203]

Now, Norton has a vested interest in *The Power of the Daleks*. But Nation had a vested interest in not liking Whitaker's stories, because they were made at exactly the moment his Dalek TV series came to nought.

---

[203] Norton, Charles, interview with author, 20 September 2016.

## Children of the Revolution

Whatever the situation with Nation, Whitaker was required to write out the Daleks, and decided to do so with a showdown on their home planet of Skaro – the first time the Doctor had returned there since the first Dalek story. That story also ended with their (apparent) destruction.

But what force could destroy them this time? In later years, **Doctor Who** would create a stalemate between the Daleks and the Doctor's own immensely powerful people, the Time Lords – but they were not introduced to the series until 1969[204], so were not an option for Whitaker.

As discussed, Nation's preference was for tough, courageous anti-Dalek soldiers of one sort or another who'd wage a hard-fought war. But Whitaker seems to have turned to the kinds of Dalek stories he'd been producing for years for the Dalek books and comic strips.

These are obviously the source of the Emperor Dalek, who makes his onscreen debut in the story but had first appeared in *The Dalek Book* in 1964. In episode 6 of the script, Whitaker describes him as 'a vast Dalek standing at one end of the [control] room.' That left Chris Thompson free to create something original; he didn't have to match the globe-headed Dalek seen in book illustrations and the comic strip. One comic-strip story had seen a battle between the Emperor Dalek and a Dalek called Zeg who started to question his orders[205]. In *The Evil of the Daleks*, the Doctor gives the humanised

---

[204] In *The War Games* episode 9.
[205] **The Daleks**, *TV Century 21* #11-17 (1965).

Daleks names, too – Alpha, Beta and Omega – and their questioning of orders leads to civil war.

Perhaps there's something of the comic strips and books, too, in the odd group of humans who witness this war. As well as the Doctor and his regular companion, there's a teenage girl (Victoria), her father (Waterfield), their friend the wrestler Kemel and mad Professor Maxtible. It's a long way from the gruff soldiers of Nation's adventures.

But the books and comic strips did not face the same budgetary restraints as the TV series – they were limited only by Whitaker's imagination and what the artists could draw. In 1978 Whitaker said:

> '**Doctor Who** emerged under great restrictions. We began production [in 1963] in the smallest Drama production studios, Studio D at Lime Grove, with an allowance of two minutes for outside filming and a budget above the line of £2,500. Each episode could have four sets and a tiny [filmed] inset.'

As we've seen, the allowance for location filming had increased by 1967, and there was a little more money per episode but, having moved to larger studios for a while, *The Evil of the Daleks* was still shot in the small Studio D at Lime Grove.

*The Evil of the Daleks* was still an ambitious undertaking. On 19 April – the day before the first filming took place on the series – producer Innes Lloyd responded to Tim Combe, who had apparently raised concerns about over-spending on the budget. Lloyd assured Combe that he – Lloyd – took full responsibility, and that costs could be recouped from two subsequent **Doctor Who** stories. But episode 7 of the story would be the last **Doctor Who** before the series took a break for the summer, and, said Lloyd, the Daleks, models and effects were all needed to make enough of an impact that viewers would return to the series in September.

To increase the sense of scale, months before Skaro was constructed at Lime Grove – for recording of episode 6 on 17 June – model filming took place on 26 April, on Stage 3A of Ealing Studios. An undated memo from Michaeljohn Harris at the visual effects department to director Derek Martinus, and copied to the visual effects team, designer Chris Thompson and Shawcraft Models, details seven shots over these two sequences – the first of explosions in the Dalek city itself, the second of a Dalek in a canyon. The shots are much more detailed than what's described in the script, suggesting Harris had something of a free hand in what would be put on screen. Two high-speed cameras would be used to capture these shots, as – Harris was keen to underscore – they could not be repeated.

Effects designer Tony Cornell shot nine and a half minutes of 8mm showing the recording at Ealing. Together with a 10-second film trim, on-set photographs and tele-snaps, we have a good impression of how this material looked in the story. As an extra on the *Lost in Time* DVD, Cornell's footage – titled 'The Last Dalek' – features commentary by Michaeljohn Harris and Peter Day – the latter also visible in the footage. 'It wasn't entirely a matter of making it up as you went along,' they say, adding that there was usually a storyboard of some sort. 'But nevertheless you got inspired by what was happening and thought of things as you went.' The high-speed cameras, filming at four times the usual speed, made the sequences look much more effective. Both men praise the set design: 'The match between model and studio scenery was pretty good.'[206]

There were still concerns that, even with these model shots to insert, the climactic war would be difficult to properly realise in studio. As a result, two more days of location filming at Ealing were arranged, this time using full-size sets and props. In the absence of Derek Martinus, who would be busy rehearsing episode 2 of the story, Tim Combe offered to direct the Ealing sequences, so long as he received a screen credit.

Chris Thompson remembers:

> 'The full-size set had to be pretty big to accommodate all the action. [...] The design course I'd done at the Royal College of Art was quite architectural in nature, so these things were just there in your mind: how to cover large spaces with a minimum amount of material.'

Given that Thompson knew his architectural history, the latticework is reminiscent of the method of building large structures with glass panes inset into prefabricated cast-iron frames. The technique can be seen in the roofs of old – but large – railway stations, and was pioneered by Joseph Paxton, who constructed a vast greenhouse at Chatsworth, a stately home in Derbyshire, and then the 'Crystal Palace' built for the Great Exhibition of 1851.

But if the technique was developed by Paxton in the 19th century, and given that some of *The Evil of the Daleks* is set in 1866, was

---

[206] 'The Last Dalek' (extra on the 2004 *Lost in Time* DVD).

Thompson designing Skaro on a Victorian basis? 'I think that's a bit of journalistic licence,' he says. 'I can't say that that would have been in my mind at all.' And then he laughs:

> 'But if it helps, I'm very willing to admit it. It was quite successful and probably a really cheap set. The money would have gone on the Emperor Dalek, which I think must have been built by Shawcraft.'[207]

Again, the script is not too specific about the action that takes place. The production team decided the fight would see Daleks exploding, revealing the blobby creatures inside. These can be clearly seen in the existing photographs from the story, and 20 years later still haunted one of the contributors to DWM's 'Nostalgia' feature – as we'll see in the next chapter.

Even so, Combe and his team had to convey a battle that would wipe out the Daleks, and had just four full-size Dalek props to work with, supplied by Shawcraft.

The next **Doctor Who** story to be made, *The Tomb of the Cybermen*, became the subject of a debate on the BBC's **Talkback** programme about the level of violence depicted. Combe doesn't remember there being any guidance on how far he might go here:

> 'I'd obviously talk it over with Derek, and maybe he talked it over with Innes. I just remember saying to Michaeljohn, "Let's have it all gooey with wires sticking out." It looked quite impressive, I thought.'

---

[207] Thompson, interview with author.

It was a suitable final end to the Daleks – except that while Combe was busy filming these sequences, the BBC had second thoughts:

> 'Innes Lloyd called me up at lunchtime on the second day. The last big explosion was due to happen after lunch [...] The explosives were ready to go boom. But Innes said to me, "I've had a word with Sydney [Newman], who's keen we carry on with the Daleks. So don't blow them all up. Belt and braces, old boy."'[208]

Newman was not the only one to question the killing-off of the Daleks. Two weeks later on 31 May, head of serials Shaun Sutton told the BBC programme review board that *The Evil of the Daleks* might be the creatures' last story, and – according to the minutes of the meeting – the BBC's director general, Huw Wheldon, 'expressed alarm'. Sutton and Wheldon agreed to investigate what was happening[209].

But it was a little late for making such a major change: reprieving the Daleks in a story specifically commissioned to kill them off for good, even as it went before the cameras. As Combe recalls:

> 'I said, "Innes, I'm all set to blow them up!" He said, "I don't know how you're going to do it but you've got to make it look like they're still alive." So I said I'd think of something. I had a chat with the cameramen and the effects people, and we fixed up a very powerful pulsating light, and hid it among all the stuff that was due to explode. I said a little prayer beforehand and then we started filming. It all blew up, but

---

[208] Combe, interview with author.
[209] Turner, *Terry Nation*, p29.

there it was – this light pulsing through all the smoke and everything, and we zoomed in on it. Roll credits. The end.'[210]

Finally, Skaro was realised in the television studio at Lime Grove, with episode 6 recorded on 17 June and episode 7 the following week. Five Dalek props were used for this last recording, again to convey a whole world going up in flames[211]. Despite the desire of the BBC executives not to kill off the Daleks for good, it seemed that 24 June might be the last time they appeared in a BBC television studio – at least for the foreseeable future.

Perhaps that's why Patrick Troughton took his 12-year-old son Michael to the recording[212]. Charlotta Martinus also remembered getting inside the Daleks[213], and it seems Lloyd took composer Dudley Simpson's daughter onto the set. It's strange to think of children clambering around the Daleks on that last day of recording, because the final episode of the story is particularly dour. Kemel and Waterfield are killed, Maxtible finally loses the last shred of his humanity, and the Daleks tear themselves apart.

Waterfield dies to redeem himself – saving the Doctor's life in the process. It's interesting that Maxtible gets to live. If we can allow the conceit of Maxtible as Whitaker's version of Terry Nation, perhaps it's fitting that he is last seen (or, today, heard) lost amid the chaos of Skaro, the Daleks burning around him after his brilliant

---

[210] Combe, interview with author.

[211] Green, Jon, and Gav Rymill, 'Evil of the Daleks: Events from Apr 67 to Jul 67'.

[212] Troughton, Michael, 'Michael Troughton's Memories', p10.

[213] 'Doctor Who Director Derek Martinus Dies Aged 82'.

scheme to use them to become rich – and hang all the consequences for everyone else – has failed.

Waterfield's death also makes Victoria an orphan with no home to return to, giving her little choice but to join the crew of the TARDIS. In the 1960s companions mostly stumbled aboard by accident, with little prospect of ever getting home again given that the Doctor could not properly control the TARDIS. Since 2005, the Doctor has had more control, enabling frequent returns to the present day so that companions can have adventures with him but maintain (admittedly strained) contact with their family and social lives. Giving the Doctor more control over the TARDIS therefore gives the companions more agency in joining him than Victoria enjoys.

If Waterfield's death helps serve Whitaker's brief to introduce a new companion, what of the death of Kemel? Like Waterfield, Kemel dies to protect his friends – but here it's not about redemption, as Kemel is already a noble character. It adds shock and drama to the final episode of the story, and perhaps it's underlining the moral in having Kemel – an exemplar of the very best of humanity, as the Doctor defined it – perfectly match a Dalek. But he could do that and survive.

It's also striking that in the very next story, *The Tomb of the Cybermen*, there's **another** mute, black character – Toberman – who initially seems threatening but then dies to save the Doctor and his friends. That duplication might have been less obvious to viewers given that *The Tomb of the Cybermen* was broadcast in September, after the summer break, but surely those working on the programme might have noticed, given that production of the stories overlapped[214].

Except that, as we've seen, there were considerable pressures on the production team, faced with recording episodes of *The Evil of the Daleks* just a week ahead of transmission. In addition, story editor Gerry Davis left **Doctor Who** during production on this story, and was replaced first by Peter Bryant and then – when he became producer on *The Tomb of the Cybermen* – by Victor Pemberton. Given these circumstances, it's easy to see why the similarity between Kemel and Toberman might have been missed. But had it been spotted, what then?

One solution might have been to combine the characters, so that Kemel joins the TARDIS at the end of *The Evil of the Daleks*, and then largely takes Toberman's role in the next story – dying at the end to save the Doctor and his friends. It would have meant introducing the Doctor's first black companion to the series some 40 years early[215]. That might have been progressive for its time, were it not for then killing him off in the next story. Would it serve the series to have a mute companion anyway? Given the complications the production team had already experienced in

---

[214] Episode 5 of *The Evil of the Daleks* was recorded in studio on Saturday 10 June 1967. On Monday 12 June, location filming began on *The Tomb of the Cybermen* and continued through the week, while Troughton, Hines and Watling also rehearsed episode 6 of *The Evil of the Daleks*, recorded in studio on 17 June.
[215] Mickey Smith, played by Noel Clarke, joined the TARDIS at the end of *School Reunion* (2006), and was heralded on the cover of *DWM* #367 as a 'bona-fide TARDIS traveller'.

introducing a new companion, would they ever have considered such a move? It seems unlikely, but thinking through these alternatives suggests why the story plays out as it does: having been transported to Skaro, Kemel has to die.

At one point, the Doctor also seems prepared to sacrifice himself and his friends rather than spread the Dalek factor through the history of the Earth. 'Five lives against a whole planet?' he says. 'Well, it's not a choice, is it?'[216]

He could have said the same thing to Jamie, when confronted about his 'callous' behaviour earlier. Jamie said that once Victoria had been rescued he and the Doctor would be 'finished', but they don't resolve that argument later[217]. It's left hanging, this sense that there's something dark and almost cold within the hero of the series. It would come to haunt **Doctor Who** in future...

## The Final End?

Of course, the Daleks weren't written out of **Doctor Who** for ever, and there never was a Dalek series. Terry Nation continued to work in British television for the next decade, before finally moving to Hollywood in the early 1980s.

In December 1967, the production team on **Doctor Who** contacted him to ask about a potential story in which the Daleks would battle the Cybermen. Nation refused permission, but did not rule out the possibility of further Dalek stories per se – suggesting he'd already given up on the Dalek TV series. The **Doctor Who** production team

---

[216] Episode 7.
[217] Episode 5.

then commissioned David Whitaker to write a Cyberman story that **didn't** feature the Daleks – *The Wheel in Space* (1968). Did he know he'd been commissioned, once again, on the basis of what Nation wouldn't allow?

On 27 March the following year, Peter Bryant – now producer of **Doctor Who** – asked John Henderson, assistant head of the BBC copyright department, to seek permission for a repeat of *The Evil of the Daleks* that summer. Whitaker had given permission by 4 April, subject to Nation's own agreement – and since the repeat began on 8 June, Nation must have agreed.

The following year, the embargo on selling the story abroad seems to have been lifted. On 10 March 1969, *The Evil of the Daleks* was sold for broadcast in Australia, later in the year it was sold to Hong Kong, and in 1970 it was sold to Singapore and New Zealand. But the ban on sales seems to have meant that it and *The Power of the Daleks* were sold to fewer countries than other **Doctor Who** stories of the period. That suggests fewer 16mm copies of the episodes were made and distributed, so missing episodes from these two stories are now less likely to be recovered than those from most other stories. It's an odd thought: Terry Nation's Dalek TV series, which was never even made, might be the reason that all but one episode of David Whitaker's broadcast Dalek stories no longer exist.

But the embargo on overseas sales wasn't the only ban to be lifted. On 12 June 1969, the Daleks finally returned to **Doctor Who**. On that day, a single specimen was in BBC Television Centre for the recording of Patrick Troughton's final episode in the lead role – *The*

*War Games* episode 10 included a roll-call of the various monsters he'd fought. It was broadcast on 21 June.

Perhaps Nation allowed this appearance because things were otherwise ominously quiet for the Daleks. In 1965, at the height of the sales of Dalek merchandise, Nation set up Dalek Productions Ltd to exploit their commercial potential – but that era seemed to have passed. On 1 July 1969 the official Registrar of Companies included Dalek Productions in a list published in *The London Gazette* of companies due to be struck off the register and dissolved in three months' time[218]. Companies were listed if the business no longer operated or didn't reply to repeated inquiries as to whether it was still operating – so even if the company was still running, things were not going well.

A Dalek was heard but not seen in episode 3 of *The Mind of Evil* (1971), and around this time the BBC's managing director, Huw Wheldon asked the **Doctor Who** production team if the Daleks could make a proper return to the series. Terry Nation was approached, and though he was himself committed to another series, **The Persuaders!**, he gave formal permission on 22 April for the Daleks to return. There were four new Dalek **Doctor Who** stories over the next four years – *Day of the Daleks* (1972), *Planet of the Daleks* (1973), *Death to the Daleks* (1974) and *Genesis of the Daleks* (1975)[219]. All but the first were by Nation, and all saw the

---

[218] 'The London Gazette, 1st July 1969.'

[219] The Daleks also make a substantial appearance in the final episode of *Frontier in Space* (1973), which leads directly into *Planet of the Daleks*.

Daleks defeated by tough, humourless soldiers of one kind or another.

But the production team felt Nation was repeating himself, and rejected his original outline for the 1975 story. They asked instead if he would present the origin of the Daleks. Ironically, he'd already outlined exactly that for the first instalments of the Dalek comic strip in 1965, which David Whitaker had then written[220]. The TV story *Genesis of the Daleks* arguably owes more than that to Whitaker. It's the first story since *The Evil of the Daleks* to return to Skaro, and we see more of its strange flora and fauna. Through the character of Davros, creator of the Daleks, we learn more of the psychology that drives them. At one point, the Doctor's companion directly questions his motives – but whereas Jamie thought him too callous, Sarah can't believe he'd hesitate in entirely destroying the Daleks. Just as in *The Evil of the Daleks* with the pulsating light, that destruction is fudged. Even Davros is exterminated in a way that allowed his return.

Ultimately, what does it take to defeat the Daleks? That's the central question. In *The Evil of the Daleks*, the Doctor is immune to the dalekising process because, he explains, 'I don't come from Earth'. As Jonathan Morris argues: 'it had already been established [in the series] that the Doctor was from another planet, and capable of being "renewed", but this is the first time it's made explicit that the Doctor is truly **alien**.'[221] Thus in a story so much

---

[220] **The Daleks**, *TV Century 21* #1-3 (1965).

[221] Morris, Jonathan and Pereira, Matthew, 'The Telesnap Archive: The Evil of the Daleks'. DWM Special edition #36 *The Missing Episodes: The Second Doctor Volume 2*.

about authenticity we glimpse something we've not seen before – the authentic Doctor.

It's more than that he's physically different to us – Jamie reveals just how little we know about him. What makes that moment thrilling, and why **Doctor Who** has kept returning to it in different forms ever since, is that for all we've come to know the Doctor, we still don't quite know what he might be capable of. The question is at the heart of *Dalek*, the episode of the 2005 series which re-established their power. It's central to 50th anniversary episode *The Day of the Doctor* (2013), and is why in *Into the Dalek* (2014) the 12th Doctor asks Clara if she thinks he is a good man.

Terry Nation took for granted that people who fought Daleks would need to be tough, ruthless and humourless. *The Evil of the Daleks* is about interrogating that assumption. Its strength, its legacy to the series still evident today, lies in making the answer uncomfortable. Yes, the Doctor loses something in fighting the Daleks on their own terms, by succumbing to the same awful ruthlessness; but they don't leave him any choice.

That is the real evil of the Daleks.

# CHAPTER 4: EARTH, 1967 TO 2017

'But sir, I heard Miss Victoria's voice!'

[Mollie][222]

In his 'Foreword' to *Henry Irving and the Bells* (1980), Marius Goring warns that there is no definitive single text of that play. Irving performed *The Bells* about 800 times between 1871 and 1905, modifying his performance over time.

It ought to be simpler with *The Evil of the Daleks*: the single, definitive text is surely the seven episodes as originally broadcast in 1967. But as the original videotapes were wiped soon after the story was repeated in 1968, it's a bit more complicated.

As we saw in Chapter 1, we can glean a lot of detail by comparing the available sources, but there are still gaps and inconsistencies. We must understand the limitations of, and biases imposed by the nature of, the sources themselves. Some sources are more readily available than others, and different sources have come to light over time. This means we have a mutable text. What *The Evil of the Daleks* is, let alone what it means, has constantly evolved in the years since broadcast. What follows attempts to chart that development.

## On-Set Photographs

For more than 20 years after the story was broadcast, the only official record available to the public was photographs taken during recording for publicity purposes. However, 'available' meant

---

[222] Episode 4.

something different before the internet. Most newspapers and magazines – and the BBC departments responsible for promoting programmes such as **Doctor Who** – were chiefly interested in new productions. Images from old programmes were rarely published.

In September 1979, more than a decade after the first broadcast of *The Evil of the Daleks*, Marvel UK launched the official *Doctor Who Weekly*, the first professional magazine devoted to the series. It originally comprised 28 pages, including two comic strips, which didn't leave much room for the nearly 16-year history of the TV series. Even so, the first issue includes a photograph from the set of *The Evil of the Daleks*: a TV camera focused on a Dalek whose top has been blown off.

Over time, *Doctor Who Weekly* became *Doctor Who Magazine* – DWM – with an increased page count and more attention paid to old stories. Even then, there was often a shortage of images. The five-page 'The Doctor Who Archive' feature on *The Evil of the Daleks* by Jeremy Bentham in *Doctor Who: A Marvel Winter Special* (1981) boasts eight black-and-white photographs from the BBC photo library. The four-page 'Nostalgia' feature devoted to the story in DWM #128 (1987) includes three photographs – less than one per page[223]. One of those images is reprinted on page 8 of DWM #200 (1993), which also boasts an 11-page 'Archive Feature' on the story with 10 further photographs – again, less than one separate image per page. Three of these images were not on-set photographs, but snapped by fan Terry Reason directly from the television screen as the story was broadcast. Before we discuss off-

---

[223] Mulkern, 'Nostalgia'.

air images, let's first address the limits of what on-set photography can tell us.

'A film may live in our memory as much through still photographs as through our experience of seeing the movie,' say David Bordwell and Kristin Thompson in *Film Art: An Introduction*[224], and the same is true of TV. As Bordwell and Thompson explain, such 'production stills' are 'typically [...] used for publicizing the film [...] and they can be useful for studying details of setting or costume.' Such stills are often taken on set during filming, but Bordwell and Thompson caution that they 'differ from what we see on the film strip. Usually the photographer rearranges and relights the actors and takes the still from an angle and distance not comparable to that shown in the finished film.'

As an example, they present a production still beside an enlargement of a frame, both with three actors stood close together. The images look similar, but the frame enlargement shows a doorway behind the actors, giving depth to the action. 'Here, as often happens, a production still does not capture important features of the director's visual style.'[225] But there's another way the on-set photographs do not tell the full story. Originally, 15 black-and-white images were released by BBC Picture Publicity in relation to *The Evil of the Daleks*. That's just over two photographs per episode, but some episodes are better covered

---

[224] Bordwell and Thompson, *Film Art*, p37.
[225] Bordwell and Thompson, *Film Art*, p38.

than others. The first six images were all taken on location at Grim's Dyke house on 24 April 1967[226]. The images are:

- '67/T1/793: A portrait of Victoria Waterfield.'
- '67/T1/794: Victoria in Maxtible's garden.'
- '67/T1/795: Victoria and Jamie waiting for an approaching Dalek.'
- '67/T1/796: Victoria and Jamie meet a Dalek.'
- '67/T1/797: A portrait of Victoria.'
- '67/T1/798: A portrait of Jamie.'

The focus seems to be the introduction of Victoria, the new companion, in episode 2. The next image is referred to as 'episode 2' and dated 20 May 1967 – the day episode 2 was recorded in the studio, where the image was taken.

- '67/T1/914: Victoria and Ruth being served tea by Mollie.'

Two photographs referred to as 'episode 6' were taken on set the day of the recording of that episode, 17 June 1967:

- '67/T1/1053: Victoria is taken before the Dalek Emperor.'
- '67/T1/1054: Theodore Maxtible in his laboratory.'

---

[226] In the BBC's filing system, they're referred to as 'episode 1' but dated 24 May 1967 – suggesting the wrong month has been entered, as that's otherwise four days after episode 1 was broadcast.

The remaining photographs are referred to as 'episode 7' or 'special effects', and are dated May 1967. These were taken during filming at Ealing Studios on 16 and 17 May.

- '67/T1/1163: A dying Dalek (filming shot).'
- '67/T1/1164: A destroyed Dalek and the damaged Emperor.'
- '67/T1/1165: The death of the Dalek Emperor.'
- '67/T1/1166: A Dalek exterminates the Black Dalek.'
- '67/T1/1167: The death of all Daleks, the final end.'
- '67/T1/1168: Filming shot of a dying Dalek.'

These publicity images don't include the colour photographs also taken during filming at Ealing, or the photographs taken by *Radio Times* (which include shots of the Daleks on the Ealing Studios street backlot – a setting not used in the story). Other photographs from the filming have subsequently come to light.

Today, the search term 'Evil of the Daleks' returns 34 images from the BBC's internal picture archive, ELVIS. Nine of these are from the location filming at Grim's Dyke, the majority different shots of Deborah Watling as Victoria, photographed in the grounds during the day of 24 April. But in the story as broadcast the exterior of the house was seen only once – at night. Other images show Watling pressed close to Frazer Hines, sometimes with a Dalek in view, representing the scenes where Jamie rescues Victoria. Again, these dramatic poses do not show events as broadcast – during the rescue, Jamie and Victoria are accompanied by Kemel, who does not appear in the photographs.

A further 22 images on ELVIS are from the filming at Ealing for the story's climactic Dalek battle. Just three photographs seem to have been taken on set in Studio D of Lime Grove, where the majority of the story was recorded. There's one of Maxtible in his laboratory and two of Mollie, Victoria and Ruth as if in conversation – again, something that doesn't happen in the story. We know two further images of Maxtible and Waterfield were taken (they're published in DWM #128 and #200) but even so this collection of images is a very partial record of the story.

A stills photographer had to be booked in advance to attend recording – and paid for – so it seems the production team focused on three things. First, there's the introduction of the new companion, photographed in costume in a picturesque setting. Such images were used in publicity at the time of broadcast, including on the front page of industry newspaper *Television Today*. Secondly, there's the Dalek battle on Skaro which would have had similar potential interest to the press. Finally, there are a few images of the story's main supporting cast. But many characters and sets – sizeable parts of the story – are not recorded at all.

Even where other on-set photographs exist, they tend to be of location filming – at Grim's Dyke house, at Ealing or at the Kendall Avenue location used in episode 1.

## Off-Air Audio Recordings

Although not an official record of the programme, some people could relive *The Evil of the Daleks* in the 1970s and 1980s by listening to audio recordings made by various fans at the time of broadcast. According to Richard Molesworth in *Wiped!*, cassettes were 'being enthusiastically duplicated far and wide, albeit dropping many generations [in quality] in the process.'[227] It's difficult to know how many people had access to such copies, and accounts differ about which stories were harder to obtain.

Patrick Mulkern, who now writes for *Radio Times*, recalls:

> 'One of the first episodes I came by, probably around 1979, was episode 3 of *The Evil of the Daleks*. A **Doctor Who** pen-pal kindly copied it for me. It was from his own recording that his father made on reel-to-reel tape, and it was from the 1968 repeat, complete with a breakdown in transmission and apology from the announcer. In those days people trimmed all the title music to save space on tapes, so it could be hard working out where one episode ended and the next began.'[228]

An off-air recording can give a better sense of the plot of a missing story than a limited number of photographs. It can also convey the pace and tone as we hear the actors' performances. But we can't always be sure who is talking, or where, or what is going on as they speak. An audio recording, in its raw form, is at its weakest when there's no dialogue – and episode 4 of *The Evil of the Daleks* begins with a five-minute fight sequence where only a few words are spoken. A poor quality recording, or a multi-generational copy, can make it even more difficult to follow events, and may include noise that wasn't part of the original programme, distorting the experience. We'll explore these issues further when discussing commercial releases of the soundtrack.

---

[227] Molesworth, *Wiped!*, p312.
[228] Mulkern, Patrick, interview with author, 10 September 2016.

## Published Plot Summaries

The 1972 book *The Making of Doctor Who*, the **Doctor Who** 10th anniversary special published by *Radio Times* in 1973, and *The Doctor Who Programme Guide* first published by Target Books in 1981 each contain short summaries of all stories broadcast up to their dates of publication[229]. For *The Evil of the Daleks*, each repeats the same error, setting the Victorian part of the story in 1867, not 1866. The *Radio Times* special also seems to think 'Maxtible' is a pseudonym used by Waterfield when in the present day. There's little mention of Ruth and Mollie.

The fact that each publication misdates the story suggests they used the same, mistaken source. At the time *The Evil of the Daleks* was being made, the production team would have issued an internal 'Drama Early Warning Synopsis' or DEWS, usually a single page giving an overview of the story, the later paragraphs noted as 'not for publication' as that would give away the ending. The DEWS for *The Evil of the Daleks* no longer seems to exist, but it would have been the main source for the internal document on how to promote and publicise the serial – copies of which survive. These also give the incorrect 1867 date, which was in the script for episode 2 used at the time of recording.

BBC TV Enterprises then produced an undated six-page document on the story, apparently after broadcast and used for selling the

---

[229] Hulke, Malcolm and Terrance Dicks, *The Making of Doctor Who* (1972). *Radio Times, Doctor Who Tenth Anniversary Special*, November 1973. Lofficier, Jean-Marc, *The Doctor Who Programme Guide Volume 1* (1981).

serial abroad. This contains an overview, seemingly taken from the DEWS, and a more detailed breakdown of the episodes. Ruth's part in the story is only mentioned in the episodic breakdown, which also includes the 1867 date.

Either the overview synopsis in this document or the original DEWS document seems to have been the source for both *The Making of Doctor Who* – where it's reformatted as a summary of the Doctor's travels as recorded by the Time Lords – and the *Radio Times* special from 1973. When *The Making of Doctor Who* was republished in 1976, it used the synopsis from the *Radio Times* special.

For *The Doctor Who Programme Guide*, Jean-Marc Lofficier thinks he worked from the DEWS document:

> 'I think it was a page and half, not a single page. Jane Judge at the **Doctor Who** production office kindly xeroxed the story sheets they had on file for each programme, which match your description of the DEWS – I didn't know that's what they were called. I never saw the story being broadcast, but that document was fine for my purposes, which was to generate a simple 15-line synopsis.'[230]

For later editions of *The Doctor Who Programme Guide*, Lofficier – and fans generally – had access to more detailed information about *The Evil of the Daleks*. From the 1989 edition onwards, the 1867 reference was corrected to 1866.

---

[230] Lofficier, Jean-Marc, interview with author, 21 September 2016.

Fan organisations also provided fact sheets and other information about old **Doctor Who** stories, if to a more limited number of readers. How was this material compiled?

For decades the most readily available record of *The Evil of the Daleks* was people's memories of it. Those who missed the programme when broadcast could ask for a summary from those who'd seen it. The 'Nostalgia' feature in DWM is an example of how this could be taken a step further: the instalment in DWM #128 collates memories sent in by six readers to reconstruct the plot of *The Evil of the Daleks*. It provides more detail than the short summaries published in the *Radio Times* special or *The Doctor Who Programme Guide*. But it also reveals some issues in relying on people's memories.

The first reader quoted – R Robinson of Nedlands, Western Australia – doesn't mention *The Evil of the Daleks* at all but refers to Troughton's performance as the Doctor more generally. Alan Turrell of Shoreham-by-Sea comments on a specific moment in *The Evil of the Daleks*, but he's hazy on the plot: 'I'm pretty sure it was at the end of episode one, when this man went behind a bookcase. I can't remember exactly what he had done...' What Turrell says he 'will always remember' is this man – Kennedy – being shot by a Dalek and the image of his face turning negative.

Elaine Crowley of Islington remembers 'being thrilled when Jamie finally rescued Victoria', while William Silver of Erdington recalls 'the most fantastic Dalek battle ever staged'. Les Short of Kardinya, Western Australia, provides a vivid description of the very moment being recorded in the on-set photograph published in the first issue of *Doctor Who Weekly*:

'Suddenly the black-capped Dalek was bathed in brilliant light. Its domed head with the attached eye-stalk was blown off and shot high into the air. It clattered upside down on the floor nearby. The remainder of the Dalek body stood motionless for a moment. Then from within bubbled a whitish froth, which bubbled over and down the casing, gathering in an ever-increasing pool on the floor below.'

There's some analysis, but largely the memories cited are of the most frightening and exciting moments. None of the readers mention Ruth or Mollie, whose roles in the story are only covered briefly in Patrick Mulkern's accompanying summary[231].

Perhaps we should expect this in a feature drawn from readers' memories, because of the way memory works. We tend to more vividly remember things that prompt strong emotions[232].

Imagine how different the feature would be were it based not on readers' memories but the on-set photographs. There would still be the focus on Jamie rescuing Victoria and the final battle between factions of Daleks. Ruth and Mollie might get more prominence because they appear in two images. But Kennedy, whose death so made its mark on Alan Turrell, would barely get a mention. The point is that the sources available to us, and how they are framed, affect our understanding of the story, and how we respond to it.

---

[231] Mulkern, 'Nostalgia', pp8-11.

[232] For more on how memory works, and its relation to **Doctor Who**, see chapter 8, 'Time and Memory' in Kukula, Marek and Simon Guerrier, *The Scientific Secrets of Doctor Who*.

In fact, very few fans wrote in to 'Nostalgia'. Patrick Mulkern recalls:

> 'The postbag wasn't bulging. Sometimes it was so thin, or the letters so unusable, that I solicited quotes from fans that I knew. On *The Evil of the Daleks* specifically, we didn't have much more to go on than what we printed. And I've only the haziest memories of watching it, on the repeat in 1968.'

So how was Mulkern able to write the three-page plot summary that accompanies the fans' recollections? By this point, he had his collection of soundtracks – but, as we've seen, they could tell him only so much:

> 'So I used to talk at length about these long-lost stories with some of my older fan friends such as Gordon Blows and Jan Vincent-Rudzki. They had clear memories of **Doctor Who** from the very beginning and would give me pointers.'[233]

It wasn't just that Mulkern's friends had good memories: they were also senior figures in the Doctor Who Appreciation Society. There had been an organised **Doctor Who** fandom since the mid-1960s, and from 1971 it was actively supported and encouraged by the series' producer. The DWAS, established in 1976, took things further, its reference department providing story information – STINFO – to members, and even advising the **Doctor Who** production team and a BBC documentary on the series[234].

---

[233] Mulkern, interview with author.

[234] For more on early **Doctor Who** fandom, see Marcus Hearn, *Doctor Who: The Vault*, pp124-5.

Jeremy Bentham wrote the STINFOs:

> 'The one for *The Evil of the Daleks* was produced for the DWAS in mid-July 1978, timed to appear as a set of four STINFOs released at that year's PanoptiCon convention in South Kensington over 12 to 13 August. It was then advertised to the rest of the society in our newsletter, *Celestial Toyroom*. Finished STINFOs were then reproduced to order by a local recruitment consultancy in Hendon Central, whose offices owned one of the then new Xerox dry-copiers. By the end of 1978, each STINFO was being ordered by between 800 and 1,000 DWAS members per annum.'

The STINFO for *The Evil of the Daleks* was not based on the BBC TV Enterprises document – which, as we've seen, contained some inaccurate details:

> 'By Easter 1978, my sources were four-fold, if you include asking my peers in DWAS, such as Jan and Gordon, whenever I hit blank spots – which was not uncommon. First there was my collection of *Radio Times* clippings, supplemented by a stack of programme synopses produced by the Royal National Institute for the Deaf which a friend of mine's uncle received on a regular basis and handed on. These were produced in advance of broadcast and, I later discovered, often derived from rehearsal scripts which did not always reflect the final edit of an episode and were careful about not revealing cliffhangers.

> 'Secondly, there was record producer and DJ Ian Levine, who was an active contributor to the DWAS in those days. As a

child, Ian tape-recorded every episode from, if memory serves, early 1965, but the tapes were expensive and he could not keep all of them. So he'd painstakingly transcribe the dialogue and action, week-by-week, into school exercise books before overwriting a section of tape with a new episode. There was less detail in the entries for the mid-Troughton period – presumably when the sheer effort of writing them was getting too much – but the entries for *The Evil of the Daleks* were still pretty comprehensive.

'But the major port of call for the STINFO project were the off-air tape recordings made by Richard Landen. Unlike Ian, Richard kept everything he taped on large reel-to-reel tapes. For *The Evil of the Daleks*, I would start by listening to these, one at a time over a series of nights, and make notes. I'd cross-reference these notes with the RNID synopses and photocopies of Ian's notes, before writing out the text destined for the STINFO.'[235]

Even a decade later, Jeremy's work was a valuable resource for writers such as Lofficier and Mulkern, who recalls:

'In the 1980s, when writing regularly for DWM, I was well acquainted with 1960s **Doctor Who** – even those episodes for which no visual record remained. I'd absorbed the detailed synopses written by Jeremy, which were like the Dead Sea Scrolls of lost **Doctor Who**. And I'd amassed a pile of cassette tapes of fair to middling soundtracks for most of

---

[235] Bentham, interview with author.

the 1960s episodes. In fact, Dudley Simpson[236] came into the office for an interview in 1985 and I had a wonderful afternoon playing him extracts from bootleg videos and audios, jogging his memory. He was delighted!'[237]

That interview was published in the DWM Winter Special (1985)[238]. But note what was happening: writers such as Bentham and Mulkern used the soundtracks and other documents **before** asking people to share their memories, ensuring more specific and detailed recollections.

It helped that there were ever more opportunities to question people who'd helped make old episodes. The first **Doctor Who** convention, held in south London on 6 August 1977, saw **Doctor Who** cast members past and present share their memories with 200 attendees. Further conventions followed, and interviews with production personnel were published in fan publications. DWM helped share such information about the series' past with a much wider audience[239].

The interviews and information published by the DWAS and DWM wasn't just of value to fans in the 1970s and 1980s: the insights

---

[236] This was erroneously reported as Patrick Troughton, not Simpson, in the first edition of this volume of the Black Archive.

[237] Mulkern, interview with author.

[238] Mulkern and Richard Marson, 'King of the Tracks'.

[239] Paul Winter, co-ordinator of the DWAS, says membership peaked in the late 1980s at some 3,000 members; Tom Spilsbury, editor of DWM, says that in the same period circulation of the magazine was between 15,000 and 20,000 per issue (Interviews with author, 18 and 14 September 2016).

gathered into production of *The Evil of the Daleks* remain a vital source for understanding the story, especially where the people interviewed have since died. This book makes use of many such sources.

However, it's striking (sometimes frustrating) that these old interviews rarely go into much detail about the stories being discussed. Today, DWM has many more pages per issue than it used to, so it was partly a question of how much space could be given to such recollections. But also, while Dudley Simpson was presented with clips from his stories, it seems that many other interview subjects had to rely on **only** their memories of work they'd done more than a decade before.

Memories are not always reliable. People exaggerate or embellish, and not always consciously. Accounts can be contradictory or even demonstrably wrong. What seems to stick in the memory is anything unusual: people joining or leaving the production team, jokes made on set that are not part of the story as broadcast, and things going wrong. Memories of working on a particular story can be coloured by whatever else might have been happening in the person's life at the time.

So memories are another partial record, very different from actually being able to watch an episode from the story. Which, finally, became possible for the general public in 1992...

## Episode 2 on VHS

By the time the 'Nostalgia' feature on *The Evil of the Daleks* was published in DWM, the BBC held a copy of episode 2. By chance, film collector Gordon Hendry bought a 16mm film print of the episode from a car boot sale at the Buckingham Movie Museum in the summer of 1983 – Hendry and the seller did not know it was missing from the BBC archives. Having been made aware of the fact, Hendry loaned the film print to the BBC in May 1987, and a copy was made[240]. Soon, a bootleg copy was circulating among fans – one fan who'd prefer to remain anonymous viewed a copy later that same year. The episode was shown at the Institute of Contemporary Arts on Monday 27 and Tuesday 28 June 1988.

The episode was made more widely available to the public when it was included on the VHS cassette *Daleks: The Early Years*, first released on 6 July 1992. This was just one in a successful range that eventually saw all the existing episodes of **Doctor Who** made available to the public. DWM #486 (2015) included the first of a four-part feature on the history of the **Doctor Who** videos, and writer Charles Norton was happy to share his research, gathered from internal BBC information and industry publications of the time:

> '*Daleks: The Early Years* was recorded to have sold more than 20,000 but less than 30,000 copies over its first five years on sale. Its highest position in the sales chart was number 5. The average lifetime sales figure for monochrome **Doctor Who** releases on VHS was about 24,000 units, averaged out across the 1980s and 1990s, while the average for colour stories across the same period was about 21,500.'[241]

---

[240] For the full story of the recovery of the episode, see Molesworth, *Wiped!*, pp229-233.
[241] Norton, interview with author.

The VHS range had a dramatic impact on the way many older stories were received and understood. Fans no longer had to rely on the memories of those old enough to have seen the original broadcast, or photographs that didn't necessarily reflect what happened on screen. In DWM and other publications of the time, we can see **Doctor Who**'s past being reappraised, with received wisdom challenged and sometimes overthrown.

But the episode released on VHS differs from that originally broadcast in a number of ways. There's a lot of dirt flickering on the screen and a notable scratch running down the frame about a quarter of the way from the left. The scratch is on Hendry's print, and the dirt and other defects are typical of archive film. The episode on VHS is also a copy of the BBC's 16 mm print, which is a copy of Hendry's 16mm print, which itself might not be a direct copy of the original two-inch videotape, and each generation of copying means a drop in quality.

To make a 16mm copy from the two-inch videotape in the first place, a film camera was positioned in front of a screen on to which the episode was played from the tape. As Richard Molesworth explains in *Wiped!*, 'the 16mm film recordings were slightly zoomed in ... to ensure that the edges of the screen were never captured.'[242] This means that the existing 16mm episode is a slightly cropped version of the original – as we'll see when we compare the version of the episode later released on DVD with the tele-snaps.

---

[242] Molesworth, *Wiped!*, pp273-4.

Secondly, the video recording system the BBC used for *The Evil of the Daleks* (and generally for studio recordings) captured images at twice the rate of the 16mm film[243]. The result is that video has a distinctively different look and feel – the image seeming 'warmer', the movement more 'fluid' than film. This is evident watching surviving TV programmes from the time where the convention was to record interior scenes in a TV studio on videotape and exterior locations on film. It's been argued that many people did not – and still don't – notice, but the difference was jarring enough to inspire a sketch on **Monty Python's Flying Circus**: 'Gentlemen, I have bad news – this room is surrounded by film!'[244]

Film copies of **Doctor Who** episodes lack video's distinctive look and feel, and the sense of immediacy it conveys. The poor quality of the copy as seen on VHS makes the episode seem that much older: an ancient artefact of a bygone age rather than, as we saw in Chapter 1, a **Doctor Who** story very much engaged in the present.

On the VHS, the episode is preceded by a two-sentence summary of the events of episode 1 and followed by a slightly longer description of how the story ends. This helps us better understand the events we witness, so we can get more caught up in the story. Though it's understandable that these summaries are kept short,

---

[243] The 16mm film captured images at a rate of 25 frames a second. The video system used interlaced fields rather than individual frames, allowing a faster refresh rate of 50 fields per second. See *Wiped!* for more technical detail.

[244] From the episode *Live from the Grill-o-Mat*, first broadcast 28 October 1970.

much of the story is left out – there's again no mention of Mollie or Ruth.

That these links are presented by Peter Davison, who played a later incarnation of the Doctor, perhaps lends authority to what he tells us. There are also interviews with some of the cast and crew, recalling funny moments from the set. Again, this all shapes our response to the story. The 'Nostalgia' feature speaks in awe of the thrilling final battle between warring factions of Daleks, but from the VHS we hear a behind-the-scenes story that undercuts that atmosphere: to relieve tension in the studio as these complex scenes were recorded, one Dalek broke into song.

## Audio Cassette Release of the Soundtrack

Having been available unofficially to fans for many years, the soundtrack of all seven episodes of *The Evil of the Daleks* was first released commercially on two audio cassettes on 6 July 1992. This was the same day as the release on VHS of *Daleks: The Early Years*, suggesting the BBC co-ordinated releases, allowing (even encouraging) buyers to relive the story as fully as was then possible.

The source for the cassette release was an off-air recording made by fan Richard Landen, who in 1967 placed the microphone of his tape recorder by the speaker of his TV set[245]. This method meant his recordings are not of high quality. Mark Ayres, who later worked on restoring the soundtrack of the episodes, explains that recording like this, 'degrades the recording, as you're recording the

---

[245] See Molesworth, *Wiped!*, pp311-13 for more details about Landen's recordings.

sound of the television itself. But you are also recording the room, and anyone in it, and perhaps cars and planes and birds outside.'[246]

Even so, the release was often still of better quality than the many unofficial versions of the soundtrack, which were multi-generational copies of either Landen's or other people's recordings. There were also notable differences.

For the cassette release, the BBC could not secure the rights to two pop songs played in the Tricolour in episode 1 – 'Paperback Writer' by the Beatles and 'Nobody Knows the Trouble I've Seen' by the Seekers. As a result, the whole scene was cut from the release. The duration of episode 1 on the cassette is 20m 23s – almost four minutes short of the broadcast version.

But the most striking difference between the cassette release and unofficial copies of the soundtrack, as well as with the programme as originally broadcast, is the addition of narration spoken by fourth Doctor actor Tom Baker and produced and apparently written by John Nathan-Turner – the producer of **Doctor Who** in the 1980s, who had worked on the programme since the late 1960s.

How does the narration shape our response to the story? Baker and Nathan-Turner both seem to have been chosen because of their connections to later **Doctor Who** – as if that lent authority. Other cassette releases of **Doctor Who** soundtracks from the same period even had narration in the first person: a future incarnation

---

[246] Ayres, interview with author, 8 August 2016.

of the Doctor recalling his past adventure, authoritatively offering new insights into what the Doctor thought and felt at the time.

However, the narration of *The Evil of the Daleks* cassette release is in the third person and rather neutral – even sparse. For example, episode 4 begins with the fight between Jamie and Kemel. The broadcast version reprises Jamie's line, 'Hullo, who are you?' from the previous week's cliffhanger and then nothing more is said until the Doctor explains, 'It took courage...', some five and a half minutes into the episode. On the cassette, the narration doesn't start until 1m 13s into the episode, where it provides just a single sentence:

> 'Jamie and Kemel fought long and hard, each one gaining the upper hand for a time, then succumbing to the strength of the other.'

There follows 1m 45s without dialogue or narration, so we're left to imagine the fight based on grunts and scuffling. Then:

> 'The Turk was enormously powerful, but it was Jamie's quick wits and wily strength that saved Kemel from falling to his death.'

We're not told what he might have fallen from or how Jamie saved him. Another 1m 37s pass without a word spoken before there's any more detail:

> 'They found themselves near the room from which Victoria had been taken, discovering her handkerchief lying on the floor. Jamie lurched forward, and this time Kemel returned the compliment and saved Jamie from being spiked by a

metal blade. The odd couple, equal on all terms, decided to join forces.'

Another 33s pass without comment, before the Doctor's first line of dialogue.

Perhaps it's better, even more authentic, not to impose much narration on the original soundtrack but, together with the quality of the recording, it can make it hard to follow what's happening.

That's not the fault of the writer of the narration, who had to piece together events from whatever other sources were available to anyone working for the BBC. John Nathan-Turner died in 2002 and there's no contemporary interview in which he discussed his approach to the narration script or the sources used to write it. But it seems those sources were limited – as John Peel explained.

## Novelisation

*Doctor Who: The Evil of the Daleks* by John Peel was published by Target Books (then an imprint of Virgin Books Ltd) on 19 August 1993. It was the last TV **Doctor Who** story to be novelised in the range which had begun in November 1964 with a retelling of the Doctor's first encounter with the Daleks. The author of that first book was David Whitaker.

That first novelisation includes illustrations based on on-set photographs from the recording of the TV story, suggesting the book is a faithful account of the story as broadcast. But Whitaker made a number of changes. For instance, there's a very different account of the Doctor meeting his companions Barbara Wright and

Ian Chesterton – something that happened on screen in a different story altogether[247].

Some later novelisations took similar liberties with the source material. Other authors saw their job as to provide an authentic record of the programme as broadcast, in the days when there seemed little chance that most people would see the episodes again. John Peel's approach fell somewhere between these two approaches and was based on his working relationship with Terry Nation. For Peel's first novelisation, of 1965 story *The Chase*, Nation provided him with early drafts of his scripts, before material was added by story editor Dennis Spooner – material Nation hadn't liked. Peel based his novelisation on this original, unbroadcast version of *The Chase*, arguing that his book is an authentic recreation of Nation's original vision.

But, as Peel says:

> 'Terry remembered very little about *The Evil of the Daleks* – he'd simply handed the assignment on to David Whitaker, and that was pretty much all his involvement […] I had the audiotapes of the episodes – quite old copies, of course, and not always easy to understand! And then there were the scripts. But we had a devil of a time getting them – the BBC were of no use at all.'[248]

According to Peel, Target Books' contact at the BBC was Peter Cregeen – but he was the BBC's head of series, with responsibility

---

[247] See Whitaker, David, *Doctor Who in an Exciting Adventure with the Daleks*, 'Chapter 1: 'A Meeting on the Common', pp1-16.
[248] 'An interview with John Peel'.

for programmes being made and broadcast (and the man who'd cancelled production of **Doctor Who** after the 1989 series). Presumably someone in Cregeen's staff was delegated to provide scripts for the novelisations, but no scripts were forthcoming, either from *The Evil of the Daleks* or from *The Power of the Daleks*, which was also by David Whitaker and which Peel was also due to novelise (it was published on 15 July 1993).

'My editor, Riona MacNamara, had a very hard time,' Peel recalls. He says MacNamara eventually made contact with June Barry, who had been married to Whitaker:

> 'June supplied us with at least four of the scripts[249]. Riona was the one who spoke to her, not me. The rest of the scripts eventually came courtesy of Jonathan V Way at DWAS. Terry didn't have copies of either story, at least not that he could find.'[250]

However, MacNamara doesn't think she was involved in these novelisations – she left Virgin Books in 1992. Her then boss, Peter Darvill-Evans, doesn't recall what happened, and neither do Rebecca Levene or Kerri Sharp, who worked on the books after her departure[251]. But Jonathan Way does:

---

[249] Circumstantial evidence suggests these were the four rehearsal scripts from *The Power of the Daleks*.
[250] Peel, John, interview with author, 14 July 2016.
[251] Darvill-Evans, Peter, interview with author, 21 September; Levene, Rebecca, correspondence with author, 14 September to 6 October 2016.

'At the time, I was involved in DWAS. We wanted to produce posters of Target **Doctor Who** book covers for our members, and I spent a lovely afternoon at the Virgin offices going through the artwork. Rebecca Levene was very kind and welcoming, and while we were chatting she said no one seemed to have these scripts. I was suitably agog – "I've got copies," I said – quietly omitting to mention that they weren't mine. I'd borrowed them from a friend, Steve Roberts.'[252]

Asked where he got them, Steve Roberts recalls:

'I was working for the BBC a few years before this. Innes Lloyd – the producer of the story – still had a BBC office. I found the address in the BBC staff directory and sent him a letter asking if I could have permission to borrow the scripts for *Power* and *Evil*, and he was kind enough to say yes.'[253]

Lloyd died in 1991, so Roberts had had the scripts in his possession for at least two years. 'They were just the standard camera scripts,' he says – the same ones later included in the box-set release on CD of the soundtrack of *The Evil of the Daleks* and other stories from the period.

Way rang Roberts to ask permission, then delivered the scripts to Virgin. He remembers:

'Rebecca was delighted. It was getting late by that stage so she had the scripts copied over the next few day, and they

---

[252] Way, Jonathan, interview with author, 3 October 2016.
[253] Roberts, Steve, interview with author, 14 October 2016.

arrived safely back with me in a great big parcel some days later.'[254]

'I have no memory of this,' Levene admits, and doesn't remember speaking to June Barry, either[255]. Barry had already been interviewed about her former husband's work on **Doctor Who** by Jeremy Bentham for his book *Doctor Who: The Early Years*, so it's possible the contact with her came through fan circles, too.

Scripts can be written right up to and during recording, and – as we saw in Chapter 1 – the first drafts of episode 1 and 2 were very different from the episodes as broadcast. But comparing Peel's novelisation to the soundtrack, there don't seem to be many differences. Peel could not locate his copies of the scripts, but the lack of variance suggests that even those received from Barry dated from close to the point of recording. Even so, given the difficulties involved in tracking down this source material, how authentic is the novelisation as a reproduction of the story as broadcast? Peel responds:

> 'Well, more so than *The Power of the Daleks*, where I invented a completely new character – the colony doctor. In *Evil*, I expanded various parts of the story, and I threw in a **Star Trek** joke, but I kept mostly to the scripts. I'd estimate about 80% authenticity.'

---

[254] Way, interview with author.
[255] Levene, correspondence with author.

That still leaves 20%, suggesting Peel exercised some dramatic licence. 'Terry always encouraged me to make the books my own, and "write what you feel you have to,"' he says[256].

## Archive Research

As well as interviewing people about their memories of old **Doctor Who** stories, a number of fans sought documentary evidence that could offer more objective insights into the programme. For example, DWM #200 – already mentioned above – includes a special instalment of 'What The Papers Said', a regular feature by Marcus Hearn exploring newspaper archives for contemporary responses to **Doctor Who**[257].

In the same issue, 'A Personal Note' presents correspondence between fan Gary Hopkins and the late David Whitaker – although there's no mention made of *The Evil of the Daleks* in particular[258]. The feature is accompanied by previously unpublished photographs of Whitaker from the personal collection of his brother Robert – who'd been reached via his son, Steve Whitaker, who at the time was an artist for Marvel UK, then publishers of DWM.

Then there is the 11-page 'Archive Feature' devoted to *The Evil of the Daleks*, written by Andrew Pixley[259]. By this time, various documents from the production of this and other **Doctor Who** stories were circulating among fans – just as fans also shared copies

---

[256] Peel, interview with author.
[257] Hearn, Marcus, 'What The Papers Said'. DWM #200.
[258] Hopkins, Gary, 'A Personal Note'. DWM #200.
[259] Pixley, Andrew, 'Doctor Who Archive Feature: Serial LL, *The Evil of the Daleks*'. DWM #200.

of soundtracks. Much of this information had been collated and analysed in *Doctor Who: An Adventure in Space and Time*, a fan publication produced by the group CMS, each issue of which was devoted to a whole **Doctor Who** story, in sequence. The issue covering *The Evil of the Daleks* was published in 1983, and was a key source when Pixley came to write his 'Archive Feature'. Newer finds added detail. In the case of *The Evil of the Daleks*, we know that some documents – such as scripts – were provided by Whitaker's family. The fanzine *DWB: The Journal of British Fantasy* #94 (1991) published five photographs showing location filming from the opening of episode 1, provided by Alexandra Tynan[260]. Sonny Caldinez was in possession of a photograph of himself as Kemel, arms crossed so we can see the leather straps around his forearms[261]. Other material seems to have been unearthed during production of a documentary about **Doctor Who**, *Resistance is Useless*, first broadcast on BBC Two on 3 January 1992, and perhaps more was discovered in preparing the cassette releases of soundtracks including *The Evil of the Daleks* later that year.

A single document could provide a wealth of new information. For example, one source for the DWM 'Archive Feature' on *The Evil of the Daleks* was the 'programme as broadcast' document – or 'PasB' – for each day of broadcast. The PasB provides information on all programmes broadcast on a given day, but for the episodes of *The Evil of the Daleks* in particular, the PasBs provide: episode production number, recording date, and tape number; episode duration; cast, including extras, and key crew; details of film

---

[260] 'Someone's Stolen the TARDIS!!'
[261] DWM Special Edition #4: *The Complete Second Doctor*, p32.

sequences – whether specially shot by the BBC or from stock, and how long those sequences run; and details of all music used – the name of the music, the musicians and its source, plus – in most cases – how much of it was used in the episode. The PasB for episode 1 tells us that as well as 1m 0s of 'Nobody Knows The Trouble I've Seen' and 1m 5s of 'Paperback Writer', there was 0m 36s of the show's theme tune, an unknown amount of 'Youngbeat' by the BBC Orchestra[262], and 5m 29s of specially composed music by Dudley Simpson, dubbed on tape and played by an ad-hoc orchestra. Today, the PasBs for *The Evil of the Daleks* are published as a PDF on the BBC's official **Doctor Who** website – with the warning that they 'were working documents and are not preserved in a pristine condition'[263].

Fan researchers were also beginning to explore the BBC Written Archives Centre in Caversham. Andrew Pixley first visited in November 1993, months after his 'Archive Feature' on *The Evil of the Daleks* had been published. But others, such as Marcus Hearn and Stephen James Walker, were there ahead of him.

The Written Archives Centre was – and is – open to researchers by appointment, though fees and other restrictions can apply. Researchers were not able to view files from programmes less than 25 years old, so much of the investigation done in the 1990s was into **Doctor Who**'s earliest years.

---

[262] In fact, this is an example of the PasB being misleading. 'Young Beat' is the title of a 1966 record. The cue is actually 'Mexican Beat by 'Jack Trombey' (i.e. Jan Stoeckart), and it's not the BBC Orchestra but the International Studio Group.

[263] 'The Evil of the Daleks', BBC **Doctor Who** website.

Today, the Written Archives Centre holds six production files for *The Evil of the Daleks* – numbered T5/2,531/1 to T5/2,531/6 – each relating to an episode of the story. A file for the seventh, final episode – presumably T5/2,531/7 – is not listed in the archive's database, suggesting a file was never passed to the archive rather than that it was but has since been lost. These files were originally created by the BBC's television registry staff, who sorted papers collected from the production department, so it's possible they mislaid a seventh file. However, the bulk of material relating to *The Evil of the Daleks* is in the file for episode 1, with less material in each subsequent file, so perhaps there simply wasn't enough material for a file devoted to episode 7.

Among the documents in the files for *The Evil of the Daleks* are: programme recording forms that detail the opening and closing moments of each episode; memos confirming various telephone conversations, mostly booking actors and equipment, or agreeing terms; copies of the covering slips sent to cast members with their scripts (and revised scripts) – the scripts themselves not included; two very short original outlines of *The Evil of the Daleks* that are very different from the final story; a number of documents confirming a change in the brief to writer David Whitaker and agreeing fees for new scripts; the schedule for the location filming complete with hand-drawn maps; details of fees paid to the cast, and supplementary payments for costume fittings and location filming; summaries of estimated costs from various departments; a series of revised budget estimates; notes on the story's selling points for use in publicity; draft copy for coverage in *Radio Times*; notes by producer Innes Lloyd intended for all production teams, directors and their assistants on **Doctor Who**; notes on costume and make-up for each member of the cast; and much else besides. Some documents are dated, while others are not. There are various duplications, including documents that are mostly but not quite the same. Some documents include the neatly typed name of the people who wrote them. Others are signed, if not always legibly, and many are anonymous.

The Written Archives Centre also holds copies of the seven camera scripts for the story – that is, the scripts used at the studio recording of each episode, detailing how the different cameras would cover the action, such as when a wide shot should cut to a close-up. We can deduce late additions and revisions to the script as they appear in a different typeface or style because they were written on a different typewriter. The sequence of scene and page numbers can also be a clue: for example, 'New page 7' implies a late amendment.

In addition, the archive includes personal files for many of the cast and crew. For example, there are four files relating to David Whitaker, covering his time both as a BBC staff member in the script department from 1957 to 1964, and afterwards as a freelance writer.

During the late 1980s and early 1990s, such material was analysed and shared in fan publications, the more mainstream DWM and a number of books on **Doctor Who**. DWM #200 and the attention it paid to David Whitaker and *The Evil of the Daleks* were part of much broader research into the history of the series. As we've heard, the 'Archive Feature' included three off-air photographs from *The Evil of the Daleks*, taken by fan Terry Reason during the broadcast of episodes 4 and 5. But soon after the 'Archive Feature' was published, a treasure trove of further such images was found.

## Off-Air Tele-Snaps

'Tele-snaps' was the name used by photographer John Cura for the still images he took of programmes as they were broadcast in the 1950s and 1960s. In the days before home recording and when broadcasters did not retain programmes as a matter of course, Cura operated a successful business selling such tele-snaps to broadcasters, the media and the cast and crew.

The system Cura devised captured images on half a frame of 35mm film so that he could take twice the number of pictures per roll. But this meant that the images he produced were small – 24mm by 18mm, or about the size of a postage stamp. He offered enlargements, but at 60mm by 40mm these were not much larger than a standard business card. As a result, his images are of low resolution and lack detail. Many of them have horizontal lines across them, an effect of photographing directly from a TV screen. Nevertheless, they provide a visual record of otherwise missing programmes.

Until 1993, tele-snaps were known to exist for only a few old **Doctor Who** stories. For example, in 1984, Jeremy Bentham interviewed Christopher Barry, director of much early **Doctor Who**, and discovered that he'd kept tele-snaps of all six episodes of *The Power of the Daleks* (1966).

By 1993, Hearn recalls:

> 'I'd been to the Written Archives Centre two or three times. I was assigned a research assistant there, Neil Somerville,

who was a lovely man. We were almost playing a game: I'd try and guess what the archive had, and he'd disappear into the stacks for half an hour, then come back and tell me if what I'd asked for was there.'

On Friday, 10 September 1993, Hearn tried another tack:

'I said to Neil, "Rather than me trying to guess what you've got, do you have such a thing as a list?" And he did. It came off a daisy-wheel printer, on sheets of paper with holes in the side. There was **Doctor Finlay's Casebook** [a BBC series from 1962 to 1971] and then **Doctor Who**, with all these files listed. Underneath a section marked "finance", there was an entry for "tele-snaps: series Z-UU" and two files. I said, "What are these?" Neil looked at it and said, "I don't know." He disappeared into the stacks and came back with these amazing, huge scrapbooks. I don't think he'd ever seen them before. He asked me what they were and I said, "These are probably the only visual representation of episodes of **Doctor Who** that don't exist any more!" It was amazing.'

Each strip of images had been glued onto pages in the scrapbooks alongside listings for the relevant episode cut from the *Radio Times*. The scrapbooks contained tele-snaps for 101 episodes of **Doctor Who**, though several were not from missing episodes while tele-snaps were already known to exist for others, such as *The Power of the Daleks*. Even so, it was a monumental find, including 383 off-air photographs from the missing six episodes of *The Evil of the Daleks*: 63 from episode 1, 61 from episode 3; 63 from episode 4; 67 from episode 5; 65 from episode 6; and 64 from episode 7.

That lunch time, Hearn went out to a pay phone to call Gary Russell, the editor of DWM, to tell him what he'd found:

> 'Our first thought was obviously how we could share these with people as quickly as possible. But bear in mind that in those days, just like we didn't have mobiles, there was nothing like affordable flat-bed scanning, let alone scanners you could carry around.'

Over the next week, an agreement was reached: Marvel UK paid for the tele-snaps from missing episodes of **Doctor Who** to be photographed, and for the resulting negatives and stills to be delivered to DWM for publication. However, the team at Marvel UK were not involved in the actual photography session, and Hearn admits that:

> '...what we got back was by modern standards pretty grotty. The quality was low and you could see the glue where they'd been pasted into the scrapbooks. That dictated how they were presented in the magazine: we couldn't print them big.'[264]

At about the same time, Stephen James Walker was working the same ground:

> 'I made about a dozen one-day visits to the Written Archives Centre between early 1992 and late 1993, carrying out research for the books that David Howe, Mark Stammers and I had been commissioned to write for Virgin. I discovered the two files of tele-snaps on one of the last

---

[264] Hearn, interview with author.

visits I made – though whether it was before or after 10 September 1993, I couldn't say. I immediately had photocopies made of the contents. After discussing the situation with David Howe over the phone I got in touch with Gary Russell to let him know about the files' existence, as it seemed that only DWM would have the clout and budget to get proper copies made so the tele-snaps could be published for all fans to see. But Gary had just been told about them by Marcus. So I think the safest thing to say is that Marcus and I discovered them independently at around the same time.'[265]

The point is that there was a small industry of researchers working their way through such archives independently, even in competition with one another, but ready to share their finds and discuss ways to disseminate them more widely.

The first set of these tele-snaps was published in DWM #207 (1993), showcasing episode 4 of *The Tenth Planet* – arguably the most missed of all missing episodes of **Doctor Who** as it features the first change of the series' lead actor. On television, *The Tenth Planet* had been followed the next week by *The Power of the Daleks*, but – as we've seen – tele-snaps from that story had already been found, and published elsewhere. So DWM #208 skipped ahead to begin serialisation of tele-snaps from *Fury from the Deep* (1968), a story from which there were very few known on-set photographs. Hearn recalls:

[265] Walker, Stephen James, interview with author, 21 September 2016.

'For those first two stories we did, the tele-snaps were just scanned in strips and a grid put over the strip to divide up the images. It was a bit of a disaster: the images were poor quality and the presentation wasn't quite right.'

Accompanying each image was a short caption, so that readers could follow the story:

'I remember on the captions for *Fury from the Deep* we had camera scripts where they existed, and we had the audio, but we had an awful time trying to figure out what was going on. Matthew Pereira, a friend who lived locally who was also a fan, helped out. He shared my fascination for these images. But it was terribly hard to get done.'[266]

Pereira spoke about the process to fanzine *Vworp, Vworp* in 2016:

'With only a ropey "nth" generation audio tape, an A4 blow-up of the contact sheet [for the tele-snaps], a magnifying glass and a tatty old Target novel, we spent long evenings trying to match the dialogue and events to the pictures. Having to condense three minutes of screen time into 26 words and still retain the narrative flow was another challenge. After we'd done a few episodes we discovered a curious anomaly – about 10 to 15 minutes into any given episode there would be a scene for which there were no snaps.'[267]

---

[266] Hearn, interview with author.

[267] Quoted in Scoones, Paul, 'Telesnapped!', *Vworp Vworp* #3, p171.

'A logical explanation for those gaps is that the camera was "locked" to the screen and Cura was busy changing a roll of film,' says Hearn.[268]

From mid-1994, Pereira took sole responsibility for providing these captions. By 1996, when the tele-snaps of *The Evil of the Daleks* were serialised in DWM #237 to #243 (1996), the format had been well established. The images are printed at 42mm X 30mm, almost twice the size of the originals, but it's still easy to miss certain details[269].

This detail is more evident when we compare the tele-snaps as published in DWM to those posted as a 'photonovel' on the BBC's official **Doctor Who** website four years later in 2000, episode by episode over six weeks (they are still there, in an archived part of the site)[270]. Such comparison also makes clear that DWM did not publish **all** the tele-snaps available. For example, the photonovel of episode 6 has two adjacent tele-snaps of Maxtible and Waterfield

---

[268] Hearn, interview with author.

[269] For example, the sixth image from episode 1 shows a lorry carrying the TARDIS passing out of the right-hand side of the frame. Despite having seen that image several times since that first publication, I'd not noticed until writing this book that we can also – just – see the Doctor and Jamie hurrying after the lorry.

[270] Some sources say the tele-snaps were published on the **Doctor Who** website in 2004, based either on the date given in the source code of the pages – 27 May 2004 – or the dates of page updates given at the Internet Archive (https://archive.org/web/). However, that's referring to when the already existing pages, and the whole of the **Doctor Who** site, were 'regenerated' using the content management system, as part of an overhaul of the site in preparation for the return of **Doctor Who** to TV in 2005.

standing close together. In the first, Maxtible's head is lowered as he draws on his cigar, in the second he turns to Waterfield. DWM published only the first of these. A little later in the same episode, the photonovel includes two almost identical images of the Dalek device that will destroy Maxtible's house; again, only the first is published in DWM.

By 1996, DWM's editor was Gary Gillatt, who had inherited the format established by his predecessor, Gary Russell. Gillatt recalls:

> 'There was a set number of spaces for pictures in the grid, so the best selection was made to tell the story. I think that in both the examples you give, you can see why one picture was chosen instead of the other.'

Another option would have been to give the tele-snaps more pages.

> 'I certainly wasn't about to do that! I wanted to get rid of them from the magazine as soon as possible, as they were very dingy and unrewarding. I argued for a summer or winter special with all the tele-snaps, but this was around the time our special issues were dropped, after Panini took over Marvel.

> 'Could they have been printed bigger with more appreciable detail? I doubt it. A special arrangement was made for the tele-snaps – again, before my time – as it blew our picture limit and was a labour-intensive process for repro. Certainly, there was no money available to have the images worked on

or enhanced for further enlargement.'[271]

Even so, the tele-snaps of *The Evil of the Daleks* published by DWM provide a wealth of detail not previously available. For example, there's the almost dialogue-free fight between Jamie and Kemel at the start of episode 4. The narration on the audio cassette describes the fight in just 96 words, but the same sequence is covered by 17 tele-snaps, for which Matthew Pereira provides captions totalling 285 words. The tele-snaps show us what Jamie and Kemel are wearing, in which rooms the fight takes place – it moves around the building – and suggests how it was framed and shot. We even get individual beats of the fight, for instance:

- 'A glancing blow catches Jamie off-guard and he falls to the floor.'
- 'Jamie twists the Turk's foot...'
- '... and sends him crashing into a chair, which shatters under the impact.'

Technology had moved on since Hearn first discovered the images. Initially, website producer Rob Francis visited the Written Archives Centre with a portable scanner in his bag, but a better series of scans was then made using a new, non-portable machine at the BBC, with the tele-snaps delivered from Caversham.

James Goss, then senior content producer for BBC Cult (the team that ran the site at the time) recalls that the tele-snaps 'were a thing of marvels, but each frame was so tiny and they were covered in Copydex' – the glue used to stick them into the scrapbooks. His

---

[271] Gillatt, Gary, interview with author, 10 August 2016.

team used the then relatively new Adobe Photoshop to best present the images:

> 'We applied a standard border as some were missing or weirdly cropped. We bumped up the [tonal] levels and repaired as many glue spatters and freckles as we could. The job went out to various team members – we didn't have any spare cash – with varying level of success. Kim Plowright and Rob Francis were by far the best, and Rob handled the ones for *The Evil of the Daleks*.'[272]

Just as DWM did not publish every tele-snap from an episode, the photonovels omit Cura's images of the opening and closing titles. However, the photonovel of *The Evil of the Daleks* includes a link to a clip of the opening titles, which the user can watch before browsing the still images. Just as with the magazine, each image in the photonovel is accompanied by a caption so users can follow the story. But on this story in particular there was a complication.

When releasing the existing episode 2 on video or the soundtrack of the story on cassette, the BBC paid royalties to rights holders such as Nation and certain members of the cast and crew. But, in these early days of online publishing, the photonovels were a less certain area. The argument seems to have been made that the more fully the web team recreated the episodes, the more a fee ought to be due. But, as James Goss said, the web team didn't have any cash.

'So they ran it without dialogue,' says Hearn. 'That was going to

---

[272] Goss, James, interview with author, 7 June 2016.

make it difficult to do and I wasn't very keen, so Rob Francis handled it.'[273]

The web pages were not as restrictive as the grid layout used by DWM, so captions could be longer. For example, where Pereira describes the fight at the start of episode 4 in 285 words, Francis uses 335. But without dialogue, the captions are drier, less vivid than those in DWM.

Given the concerns about royalties, to what extent does the photonovel recreate the experience of watching the original episodes? Working through the images online, the poor quality is very evident. There's the low resolution, the horizontal lines, and the effects of glue. Many images are blurred, at least to some degree, because Cura was capturing movement. We'll explore how much Cura's system might have cropped the picture as broadcast, shortly.

But the main issue is how little of each episode is documented by these photographs. The original two-inch videotape on which **Doctor Who** was recorded was made up of 50 half-frames or fields per second. Episode 1 of *The Evil of the Daleks* was 24m 07s duration, or 1,447 seconds, so comprised an estimated 72,350 fields. Even on film running at 25 frames per second – such as the 16mm copies of the original videotapes – that is still some 36,175 frames. There are just 57 tele-snaps from episode 1 on the BBC website: a tiny proportion of the whole.

The presentation of the tele-snaps also affects our response. The

---

[273] Hearn, interview with author.

title page boasts coloured versions of some tele-snaps – one from each episode – which we could argue is inauthentic but little different to the cover of the novelisation also being in colour. Otherwise, the tele-snaps are presented in their original black and white.

The photonovel was published in weekly instalments – just as the original episodes had been broadcast week by week. It also presents a tele-snap at a time, each image a relatively small 240 X 255 pixels with an explanatory caption underneath. Clicking a button leads the user on to the next image and caption – so, just as with the original broadcast, we don't know what's coming next, and focus only on what is in front of us.

There is also an option to view a 'big' version of the image, presented at 800 x 600 pixels. That is still not a huge size but, as Goss explains:

> 'In 2000, that was the standard screen resolution size. Also, there didn't seem much point in running them any larger as the original frames were so small and drawn from a source that was, with 405 lines on the TV screen, by definition 405 pixels high.'

By (almost) filling the screen, the 'big' images best replicate the story as broadcast. But as presented, they don't include the captions and there's no button to click directly to the next big image – the user must click back to the standard-size image and caption to continue following the story. Clicking through the images one at a time increases the number of individual page views – a key way in which the success of websites was measured at the time. Goss adds:

'Also, there was page weight. At the time, because of most people's connection speeds, a main BBC webpage could be a maximum of 55kb including everything – so you just couldn't put 70 images of 320 X 240 pixels on one page.'[274]

Despite these restrictions, a 'contact sheet' is also provided for each episode: a single page with all the images and captions, the images presented at a very small 100 X 75 pixels. At that size, it's difficult to make out much of what is shown, though each image and caption links directly to the standard-sized image. So, although there are options to view the story all on one page or to see larger versions of the images, each directs us back to the standard view, the relatively small images framed within the page layout of the **Doctor Who** site. That means we view the black-and-white images over blocks of dark blue and green, under a banner showing Paul McGann's Doctor from *Doctor Who* (1996), and bordered by links to other parts of the site.

This all affects our response to the story. Compare the experience of listening to the soundtrack – narrated or otherwise. There, the dialogue and sound effects prompt us to imagine what events must look like. That might not be an authentic imagining – we might not base it on photographs or the existing episode from the story – but it can seem very vivid. We respond to the actors' performances, to the emotion and drama. Audio is an immersive medium: it's easy to get caught up in the story.

The tele-snaps and how they are presented make for a more remote experience. We see how the story was staged and

---

[274] Goss, interview with author.

composed, but it's harder to lose ourselves in the drama. The photonovel also includes prominent links to an introduction to *The Evil of the Daleks*, a guide to the story and a gallery of 12 behind-the-scenes photographs – reminding us that it's a work of fiction. With the links to, and images from, other **Doctor Who** stories and how they were made, there's a distancing effect. At the time the photonovel was first published, that effect was enhanced by being viewed on a computer, though today we're more used to viewing television programmes and web pages on the same devices.

In December 2013, DWM republished the tele-snaps from *The Evil of the Daleks* in DWM Special Edition #36 *The Missing Episodes: The Second Doctor Volume 2*, this time with some restoration of the images. DWM designer Peri Godbold explains the restoration process, starting with a new, high-resolution scan of the tele-snaps:

> 'Basically, it was a case of copying and pasting each frame to a separate Photoshop document, balancing the greys as they generally need a bit of boosting at the dark end, sharpening them carefully and then cleaning up any speckles and blemishes. A lot of the tele-snaps I've seen reproduced elsewhere are very contrasty – whoever did them probably used an auto-levels button in Photoshop which can destroy detail in the paler and darker ends of the spectrum.'

As in 1996, the images were printed at a size of 42mm X 30mm, but Godbold says they could have been printed larger:

> 'There is an absolutely cracking set of tele-snaps for *The Evil of the Daleks*. Not all the tele-snaps are as good. The *Evil* ones are also much sharper than a lot of the others, so some of the frames can be used quite large with a bit of

treatment. Close-ups are generally the best. It's always best to print pics at as near to actual size as possible, so these were all processed at that size.'[275]

The same grid layout was used as before, which meant, again, that some tele-snaps were omitted. Godbold's fellow designer on the magazine, Paul Vyse, says:

'...these decisions had been taken years ago, when the original tele-snap archives were printed in DWM. These new volumes were just a cleaned-up re-visiting of those.'[276]

A digital edition of this collection of tele-snaps is available[277], offering sharper but smaller versions of the tele-snaps than the photonovel – but not all of them. There are apparently no plans for DWM to re-publish the tele-snaps in larger size, or for the BBC website to publish better quality versions, or for either to include the other 31 off-air photographs from the story taken by other people than Cura.

## CD Release of the Soundtrack

The relatively low quality of the cassette releases of **Doctor Who** soundtracks in the early 1990s, including that of *The Evil of the Daleks*, prompted fan Graham Strong to contact the BBC about his own recordings. In the 1960s, he'd wired up a direct electrical connection between his TV set and a Philips EL3548 recorder – 'Just as now you would connect a CD player to an amplifier,' explains

---

[275] Godbold, Peri, interview with author, 6 June 2016.
[276] Vyse, Paul, interview with author, 7 June 2016.
[277] See 'DWM Special 36: The Missing Episodes – The Second Doctor Volume 2'.

Mark Ayres. 'So he was recording, directly, the electrical signal as originally set to tape and then transmitted.'[278]

Strong's recordings were used as the basis for a relaunch of the soundtrack releases, now on CD, beginning with the release of the 1966 story *The Massacre* on 2 August 1999. More stories quickly followed, and a narrated CD soundtrack of *The Evil of the Daleks* was first issued on 3 November 2003 as part of a set with the soundtrack of *The Power of the Daleks* and a Radio 4 documentary, *My Life as a Dalek*[279]. The soundtrack of *The Evil of the Daleks* was then released individually on 2 August 2004, and again as part of the *Doctor Who: The Lost TV Episodes – Collection Four* set on 2 February 2012, the latter including scans of the camera scripts for the episodes.

The CD release of the soundtrack is narrated by Frazer Hines. It has been reported that new narration was needed because the recording of Tom Baker's links for the cassette release had been lost. However, Michael Stevens, who was then creative writing manager at BBC Audiobooks and in charge of the range, disagrees:

> 'The Baker links wouldn't have been considered for the 2003 release, regardless of whether or not they could be located. By that time, we'd already released 16 lost stories in this

---

[278] Ayres, interview with author. See Molesworth, *Wiped!*, pp316-19 for more details about Landen's recording.

[279] Presented by **Doctor Who** writer and actor Mark Gatiss, *My Life as a Dalek* was first broadcast by Radio 4 at 11.30 pm on Tuesday 29 July 2003. It featured interviews with cast and crew from several Dalek stories.

way, predominantly narrated by Peter Purves, Anneke Wills or Frazer – so it was always going to be his gig.'[280]

The style of the narration had also been established by the first CD release. 'I knew with *The Massacre* that Peter Purves was going to narrate it,' says Sue Cowley, who wrote the narration script for that and for *The Evil of the Daleks*, among others. As we've seen, some cassette releases were narrated in the first person, and Purves had played the first Doctor's companion Steven Taylor in *The Massacre*:

> 'So I did think, "Could he do it as Steven telling the story?". But there are a lot of scenes in the story that Steven isn't even in, so that would have caused issues. I'd have had to invent some way round that – "The Doctor later told me…" It was much simpler to do the narration in the third person, and that set the precedent for the stories that came after. One or two stories might have better suited first-person narration – *The Evil of the Daleks* might be fun from Jamie's point of view – but the style had been set. We weren't just doing one-off stories, remember, we were being consistent as a series.'[281]

The narration wasn't 'in character', but Michael Stevens explains why the team felt the CDs should be narrated by the actor playing the companion:

> 'It's the traditional role of the companion to help the audience through the story – to almost be their representative on the scene. Even though the soundtrack

---

[280] Stevens, Michael, interview with author, 5 August 2016.
[281] Cowley, Sue, interview with author, 18 August 2016.

narration is in the third person, it's somehow fitting to have the companion assuming the role of that objective observer. On a more practical level, fans of the series are undoubtedly drawn towards a new recording that's been graced with the presence of a legendary companion, so it will also have been a commercial decision.'[282]

If Tom Baker lends authority to the narration on the cassette release of *The Evil of the Daleks* because of his connection to **Doctor Who**, Peter Purves, Anneke Wills and Frazer Hines arguably lend **more** authority for having been in the stories they're narrating. Did that mean they were able to point out any errors in the narration script, or at least suggest ways to make it closer to the original production? Mark Ayres recalls:

'Yes, Frazer would come up with suggestions. But they were more about phrasing if there were things tripping him up. *The Evil of the Daleks* is seven episodes and we recorded the narration in one day. Obviously, you're fitting the narration around the existing dialogue and effects, so you've got to get timings right. I had a multi-track system on the computer, with the audio from the episodes marked up so I could skip to the next gap needing narration. And I would have gone through Sue's narration script before that. They were always brilliant scripts but I had more experience of fitting narration round precise timings, so I would have done an edit. And that meant I'd go to the recording sessions knowing it backwards. We didn't have time to listen to the

[282] Stevens, interview with author.

whole story, so we'd skip ahead to each piece of narration, I'd play a bit of the soundtrack and ask Frazer to read the script. Then we'd make sure it fitted, and I could say "The intonation needs to be more like this." He might say, "Well, that doesn't sound very natural," but I'd say, "Trust me, it will after what we'll have just heard." It was actually quite relaxed, recorded at his home with no pressure from anyone else, as you sometimes get in a studio. But it wasn't really done in a way where he'd say, "Well, when we did it on the programme, it was actually like this..."'

The CD includes an interview with Hines, his memories colouring our response to the story.

Cowley is too young to have seen the original broadcast. Her primary source for writing the narration, she says, was the camera scripts provided by the BBC Written Archives Centre. Stevens recalls:

> 'When we began the CDs, Mark, Sue and I were reliant on smeary, faded black-and-white photocopies of scripts taken from microfiche film. Sometimes they were barely legible! That didn't help with making sense of the camera directions and so on.'

Cowley adds:

> 'Those were generally good for matching what was happening to the soundtrack. But *The Evil of the Daleks* was the first one I worked on where there were extended

periods with an awful lot happening on screen and the script wasn't helpful. It would just be "Jamie and Kemel fight."'[283]

Her script for the fight is markedly different to what had been available before. On the CD, the narration starts even as the opening theme tune can still be heard:

'Jamie is facing a huge and silent aggressor.'

The narration pauses, allowing us to hear the original dialogue as Jamie asks, 'Hullo, who are you?' Then, over the sounds of the struggle, the narration continues:

'Kemel steps forward, his arms outstretched, and Jamie realises that he'll have to fight this man. He darts under Kemel's arms, trying to unbalance him. Kemel seizes Jamie's fist and squeezes hard.'

The narration pauses again, this time around someone's gasp of pain – which the narration then quickly explains:

'Gasping in pain, Jamie rams his shoulder into Kemel's stomach. The wrestler staggers back and Jamie wrenches his hand free, pulling away. The two men circle each other warily. Jamie suddenly dodges left, then twists back and elbows Kemel hard in the stomach. Seemingly unaffected, Kemel lashes out, his fists catching Jamie a glancing blow that sends him reeling back.'

It's at this point, 1m 19s into the soundtrack, that on the cassette release there is the first, single-sentence line of narration. The

---

[283] Cowley, interview with author.

cassette describes the whole fight in 96 words, DWM's captions for the tele-snaps in 285 and the online photonovel in 335. Cowley's narration of the same sequence is 702 words long – roughly half the length of the description of the same events in Peel's novelisation.

It's not just that there's **more** narration; it's much more detailed, explaining the fight moment by moment. The fact it's in the present tense also makes it more immediate, a live event happening right now rather than something from history. The effect is to make the fight – and the story – more vivid. Cowley laughs:

> 'I wrote a novel! But particularly with this fight, if you just listened to the soundtrack you had no idea what was going on – there are odd grunts and things crashing about. But there's a story being told, just without any dialogue. Jamie and Kemel are enemies and by the end of the fight they are friends. So I listened to the soundtrack an awful lot. I zoomed into those tele-snaps on the website as closely as I could to glean as much as possible. There are two pictures that show Kemel has gone off the roof, but how does that happen? What is the difference between those two images in terms of action? How much time passed between them?'

Cowley admits to using dramatic licence: 'I definitely did with the fight. I had to: it had to be described. I was thinking, "As a radio play, does this make sense?"'

Cowley also made use of John Peel's novelisation, and recalls emailing Marcus Hearn about the story more generally. 'There were other stories where I spoke to Andrew Pixley. But to be honest, with *Evil*, I was so locked into it and there wasn't much time...'

Cowley began work on the narration on 5 January 2003, immediately after delivering narration scripts for *The Power of the Daleks*. Her sixth and final revisions to the scripts for *The Evil of the Daleks* were delivered just seven weeks later, on 25 February: 'And I was doing it freelance, around my full-time job. And there were other issues going on at the same time, like the music clearances.'[284]

Whereas the entire Tricolour scene in episode 1 had been cut from the cassette release of the soundtrack, this time it was included. The BBC gained clearances for the song 'Nobody Knows the Trouble I've Seen' but not for 'Paperback Writer'. Mark Ayres was able to extract the song from the scene and replace it with another from the period – 'Hold Tight' by Dave Dee, Dozy, Beaky, Mick & Tich. With the scene included and the replacement song aptly chosen, it's as authentic as could be. Ayres explained on the website of the unofficial Restoration Team responsible for restoring old **Doctor Who** episodes that:

> 'It is the policy always to present the episodes as close as is possible to their original form [...] But, as we have seen, changes occasionally have to be made for legal and/or rights issues, and such an amendment was made for *Evil*.'[285]

---

[284] Cowley, interview with author.
[285] See Question 6.3 on Williams, Ian, 'Frequently Asked Questions (FAQ) Page'.

As with the releases of old **Doctor Who** episodes on DVD, the opening and closing titles on the original soundtrack recording were replaced with 'clean' versions for the CD. 'That was a standard replacement,' says Ayres. 'Those were the only deliberate changes. I also saved a version with the original music on it, just in case.'

In 2010, a new recording of the soundtrack for *The Evil of the Daleks* and other **Doctor Who** episodes was discovered. John de Rivaz had – like Graham Strong – made a direct electrical connection between his TV set and recording equipment, but then over the years continued to experiment and modify his system. The recordings have not all been catalogued, but some are of better quality than the Graham Strong recordings (while others are worse). If his recording of *The Evil of the Daleks* proved to be better, and given what we've learnt about the story in the last 14 years, is there the potential for a new release of the soundtrack with a revised narration script? Mark Ayres considers:

> 'John's recordings are unique. I've only recently completed having a tape machine specifically modified so that it can actually play them, and I'll be working on the transfers soon. However, the Graham Strong recordings of *The Evil of the Daleks* are very good and it's unlikely we'll find better unless studio recordings suddenly appear. But you never know... Either way, if we were to release *Evil* again, I would certainly give the soundtrack another go. Technology, and my own

experience, has improved massively in the last few years. There's not a lot I would do differently, just better.'[286]

Perhaps for such a release the rights could be cleared to use 'Paperback Writer', making the complete soundtrack available to the public for the first time. But even a complete soundtrack can reveal only so much about a story we can no longer see.

For example, all the episodes of *Galaxy 4* (1965) were missing when a narrated soundtrack was released commercially in 2002. Then, in 2011, episode 3, 'Airlock', was returned to the BBC and released on DVD in 2013[287].

Before the DVD release, Gary Gillatt was able to review the episode for DWM, describing it as 'full of sharp little pleasures'. As he says, until then there had been only one known image of the monstrous Rills, which had been 'long spoken of in reverential tones by those who remember *Galaxy 4* from broadcast [...] the reality proves less awe-inspiring.' But Gillatt finds plenty of compensations: in the performance of William Hartnell, in the stylish sets and in the direction by Derek Martinus. Praise is heaped on a flashback sequence – rare in early **Doctor Who** – and a speech by the villainous Maaga:

> 'Martinus moves in for a tight close up. Maaga's face fills the screen. And then for a minute – a whole minute – she

---

[286] Ayres, interview with author.

[287] 'Airlock', and a reconstruction of the rest of *Galaxy 4*, are included on the special edition DVD of *The Aztecs*, released on 11 March 2013.

delivers a soliloquy straight down the camera lens, looking us right in the eye.'

Gillatt concludes, from being able to see the performance and the way it is directed, that this 'electrifying moment [...] deserves to lift Maaga from the rank of "forgotten" **Doctor Who** characters into the pantheon of great **Doctor Who** villains.'[288]

Martinus went on to direct *The Evil of the Daleks*, so what similar flourishes, visual jokes and details of performance and design – in short, what richness – are we missing by not being able to see the story?

## DVD Release of Episode 2 and other Existing Footage

Episode 2 of *The Evil of the Daleks* was included as part of the *Lost in Time* collection of 'orphan' **Doctor Who** episodes from different incomplete stories, released on DVD on 1 November 2004.

Most of the episodes in the collection have been painstakingly remastered and restored to look more as they did on original broadcast – in line with the Restoration Team's stated aims. This includes making a new, better transfer from Gordon Hendry's 16mm film print of episode 2. The picture and sound have been optimised, dirt and sparkle removed, and even the vertical scratch is much less apparent[289].

More strikingly, a software-based system called VidFIRE has been applied to return the look and feel of the original video recording.

---

[288] Gillatt, Gary, 'The Underwater Menace episode 3 & Galaxy 4: Airlock'. The original review was published in DWM #443.
[289] Roberts, Steve, 'Lost in Time: DVD Boxset'.

As we've seen, video ran at 50 fields per second, but film at 25 frames per second – so it was more than just a question of converting film frames to video fields. 'VidFIRE took field one from the actual film frame and field two from an estimated frame,' says Steve Roberts of the Restoration Team. This estimated frame was created by retaining elements that were the same in the film frames immediately before and after, and by then calculating and matching the paths of moving objects.

The restoration also added new, clean opening and closing title sequences – as with the CD release soundtrack. For the DVD, this means the original lettering, which would have been printed using metal typeface fonts, has been replaced with words generated on computer. The overall effect is impressive but with these titles and VidFIRE creating new frames, more than 50% of what we see on the episode available on DVD is newly generated material. It might **seem** more authentic, but it's a clever forgery. The running time of the episode is also 25:09, four seconds shorter than the BBC's official listing for the episode of 25:13. Roberts says:

> 'We've found on many occasions that the timings reported in the [PasB] documents the BBC used to record these things are not accurate when compared with unedited recordings. Secondly, back then we may still have been cutting out "dirty" frames on shot changes from the film recordings, which over the course of an entire episode would add up to a few seconds. I've no reason to believe that the BBC's copy of the episode is edited.'[290]

---

[290] Roberts, interview with author.

The unrestored version of episode 2 of *The Evil of the Daleks* included on the VHS release isn't more authentic for not having been restored or VidFIREd. It has poorer quality sound and picture, and the damage to the film is more visible, so appears less like the original broadcast version would have.

How close does the DVD restoration come to how the episode would have looked on the original two-inch videotape? No 1960s episodes of **Doctor Who** survive on their original two-inch videotape to compare it with, but **The Forsyte Saga**, the first broadcast of which overlapped with *The Evil of the Daleks*, was retained by the BBC in its original format before being digitised, and is now available on DVD[291]. Peter Crocker from the Restoration Team explains:

> '**The Forsyte Saga** was the last major BBC Two drama to be made in black and white. It survives as digital copies of the original tapes. And yes, this is what **Doctor Who** would have looked like from its original videotape, at least from *The Enemy of the World* [1967-68] onwards. Before that, **Doctor Who** was recorded on 405 [rather than 625] lines, which is not markedly different but just a little softer and less detailed. I think some of the better-quality episodes restored with VidFIRE get into the ballpark, but original videotape still has more punch and vibrancy.'[292]

---

[291] *The Forsyte Saga: The Complete Series* (1967), BBCDVD 1487, released 23 August 2004.
[292] Crocker, Peter, interview with author, 22 July 2016.

Comparing *The Evil of the Daleks* to **The Forsyte Saga**, the latter offers a cleaner, clearer image with more detail evident and slightly smoother movement. The effect is that the drama seems more immediate and fresher – as if, although it's in black and white, it has just been recorded. *The Evil of the Daleks* feels older, more distant from us: a historical document.

We can also compare the episode to tele-snaps in an effort to see how much the frame was cropped in making the original 16mm film copy from the two-inch videotape. This is not easy with the small versions of the tele-snaps printed in DWM or published online, but the editors of DWM kindly provided me with high-resolution scans of the tele-snaps for this purpose.

In a close-up of Kennedy staring at the Dalek, the tele-snap shows a slight gap between the top of his head and the upper edge of the frame, while in the episode on DVD the very top of his head is out of frame. The bottom right-hand corner of the tele-snap crops Kennedy's hand, slightly more of which is visible in the episode. In another image, we can see more of the upper-most hexagon on the panel behind Kennedy than we can in the episode. It's about 2% from the top and about 1% of the bottom from the total height of the tele-snaps[293].

Roberts says:

> 'The amount of image crop in a film recording is variable. Mostly you'll find that there is more cropped from the top than the bottom – as demonstrated in your comparisons.'

---

[293] See comparisons at Guerrier, Simon, 'Off Air Images from *The Evil of the Daleks*'.

But he also offers a different reason for the cropping effect.

> 'The film recorder camera had to ideally pull-down the next frame – pulling out the registration pins, accelerating it from stationary, decelerating it back to stationary and putting in the registration pins again – in the 1.6 milliseconds of video field blanking. This was extremely difficult and in practice it wasn't actually possible, which would result in distortion at the top of the image as the first few lines were being recorded to film as the film was still settling to stationary. To avoid this distorted area being seen on subsequent projection, the film recorder would blank the first few lines of the picture so that they were never recorded to film.

> 'There are so many variables. Cura's monitor would be over-scanned, too, there would be some overscan and blanking in the film recorded, as discussed, and there's always some overscan at the telecine stage – where film recorded on location is played into the studio recording of the episode – to avoid the ragged edges of picture appearing in the video frame.'[294]

So the existing episode is missing material from the top and bottom of the frame, but we can't be sure how much is missing, and some of it might have been missing on the original two-inch videotape.

These might be only minor differences, but they underline the point that the episode on DVD is not quite the episode as broadcast. Earlier chapters discussed how Derek Martinus

---

[294] Roberts, interview with author.

composed and framed sequences, but the surviving episode isn't an entirely accurate record of that composition and framing.

In addition to episode 2, a tiny amount of other footage survives from *The Evil of the Daleks*. Another existing episode, *The Wheel in Space* episode 6 (first broadcast 1 June 1968), includes the scene from the end of episode 1 of *Evil* and repeated at the start of episode 2, where Kennedy is exterminated by a Dalek. Close comparison shows that the footage used in *The Wheel in Space* contains three more frames – or 0.12 of a second – than in *The Evil of the Daleks* episode 2, as Kennedy moves with his back against a wall. The likeliest explanation for this tiny difference is that the footage in *Wheel* was copied from the now lost episode 1 of *Evil*, which contained a very slightly different edit of the sequence.

Included in the *Lost in Time* DVD set, this episode of *The Wheel in Space* has been remastered, restored and VidFIREd, so we face the same issues of authenticity. An unrestored version was included on the VHS cassette, *Cybermen: The Early Years*, released in 1992.

Two further pieces of footage might survive from the story as broadcast. Three seconds from episode 7 might be included in a surviving 10-second sequence from the model filming on the story[295]. The full sequence shows two hands readying toy Daleks, which then move forward through the model set of Skaro. However, as this is a film trim the material used in the broadcast episode may have begun exactly where this sequence ends. To date, this material has not been included on a commercial release. Secondly, the camera scripts and other paperwork suggest that

---

[295] 'The Evil of the Daleks Film Trim'.

episode 1 began with an establishing shot of Gatwick Airport. As discussed in Chapter 1, the production team didn't film at Gatwick for this story, so the footage might have come from the location film shot for the preceding story, *The Faceless Ones*, some of which survives.

In contrast to the VHS release, episodes on the DVD are presented without introduction. As a result, we are more removed from the characters and events on screen, so perhaps our attention is more drawn to how scenes are designed, framed and shot.

## Further Off-Air Photographs

In January 2012, 31 off-air photographs from *The Evil of the Daleks* deriving from sources other than John Cura's tele-snaps were published in issue 3 of *Nothing at the End of the Lane: The Magazine of Doctor Who Research and Restoration*. Of these, 26 came from Chris Thompson; his images are all from episode 1.

Thompson says he didn't know about the tele-snaps offered for sale by John Cura until 1993, when he was shown them while recreating the Skaro sets for a documentary, *Thirty Years in the TARDIS*:

> 'It was complete coincidence I was working on that. They gave me these photographs and said, "Can you reproduce this?" I said, "I should be able to: I designed it!"'[296]

Like Cura, Thompson took his photographs directly from a television screen as the episode was broadcast. On the day of the first broadcast of episode 1, 20 May 1967, Thompson and the rest

---

[296] Thompson, interview with author.

of the production team were busy setting up the studio recording of episode 2 later that evening, so he probably took the photographs on 8 June 1968, when the episode was repeated.

Thompson took fewer images of episode 1 than Cura because Cura's system used half the film strip – allowing him to double the number of images per roll. But using the full width of the film strip means that Thompson's images are larger. As Richard Bignell, editor of *Nothing at the End of the Lane*, describes them:

> '...they're fairly decent quality, although the scan lines from the 405-line television are very evident. All the images were in good condition, as the negatives had been kept in their folder. [Thompson] kindly loaned me the negatives so I could take high-resolution scans. A little work using Corel Photo-Paint – which is similar to Photoshop – was done to take out any blemishes caused by dust or hairs when scanning, and then a bit of balancing on the levels was done to try to bring out the best in each frame. I published all of them, and if Cura had taken a virtually identical one, I included that as well.'[297]

Comparison of Thompson's images with the tele-snaps suggests that Cura often focused on close-ups of actors' faces – perhaps actors were then more likely to buy them. Thompson's images are more often of wide shots. He explains:

> 'That was the record I wanted to keep, of the sets that I designed. But I find those photos really disappointing,

[297] Bignell, Richard, interview with author, 6 June 2016.

because the TV picture quality then was so poor, with however many lines it was on the screen. It wasn't like taking a picture of the actual sets, which I wish I'd done.'[298]

Thompson **did** take pictures of the sets built for Dalek planet Skaro, which might explain why he didn't feel the need to photograph later episodes of the story. These behind-the-scenes images were also published in the same issue of *Nothing at the End of the Lane*.

Of the other off-air images published in the issue, three were those taken by fan Terry Reason and previously published in DWM #200. One shows Maxtible on the floor in front of a Dalek in episode 4, and another is a close-up of Maxtible's face in episode 5. Both are almost identical to images among the tele-snaps. While this means we do not gain new information, we can create two-frame animations that suddenly bring something of the lost episodes back to life[299].

The third of Terry Reason's images shows Jamie and Kemel facing one another as they agree to join forces early in episode 4, and is not like any of the tele-snaps. Two images from the end of episode 5, of the Doctor and the humanised Daleks playing 'trains', were taken by Gordon Lengden and in the possession of Tony Clark, who gave permission to Bignell to publish them. Again, neither of these images are like any of the tele-snaps.

These 31 images have never been published together with all the tele-snaps, and to do so could be problematic. The tele-snaps are in

---

[298] Thompson, interview with author.
[299] See examples at Guerrier, Simon, 'Off Air Images from *The Evil of the Daleks*'.

strips and Thompson's negatives in sequence, so we know the order of the images in each set. But collating the sets can be difficult – as we saw in Chapter 1.

## Reconstruction and Animation

A number of attempts have been made to reconstruct *The Evil of the Daleks*. In 1997, Richard Develyn completed a version using Graham Strong's soundtrack and scans of the tele-snaps, but this version was never released. Develyn then worked in collaboration with Michael Palmer and Robert Franks as part of a group called Joint Venture, using better quality scans of the tele-snaps. A video of this reconstruction was made available to fans from May 1998. It included a BBC continuity announcement before the start of episode 1 and a new interview with Deborah Watling, recorded by Franks at the Nine Lives of Gallifrey One convention in Los Angeles in February that year. (Franks showed Watling part of his team's reconstructions of two other missing **Doctor Who** stories, *The Web of Fear* (1968) and *Fury from the Deep*, to prompt memories from her.) Some versions of the tape also included footage from the filming at Ealing Studios of the climactic Dalek battle, material later included on the *Lost in Time* DVD[300].

From 25 to 28 October 2006, a stage adaptation of *The Evil of the Daleks* ran at the New Theatre Royal, Portsmouth, starring Nick Scovell as the Doctor[301].

---

[300] Hugh M Pearson, *Doctor Who Reconstructions: The Lost Lords of Time – Recons, Volume One (2014)*, pp278-284.
[301] 'The Evil of the Daleks Stage Show'.

The fan group Loose Cannon released a video in January 2009 that matched Graham Strong's soundtrack from the original broadcast – without narration – to visual material including tele-snaps and on-set photographs as well as pictures edited from other **Doctor Who** stories and many other sources. There was also newly created CGI animation of the Daleks, and footage specially shot at Grim's Dyke house – the original location – with a full-sized Dalek and a double of the Doctor's companion Victoria. The reconstruction includes a short feature on the production of the story, and interviews with Sonny Caldinez and John Peel. Colin Baker – who played a later incarnation of the Doctor but also knew Patrick Troughton personally – provides an introduction and a short interview.

Other fans have also used CGI to animate sequences from the story, such as Chris Chatterton and Gavin Rymill. These can be found online[302].

On 5 November 2016, an animated version of another missing story, *The Power of the Daleks*, was made available for download from the BBC Store, with a DVD release on 21 November. When the project was announced two months before this, producer and director Charles Norton described it as 'the most ambitious **Doctor Who** archive restoration ever attempted'[303]. Surely, having created files of drawings to animate Daleks and also the Doctor as played by Patrick Troughton, it would make sense to follow up this project with a full animation of *The Evil of the Daleks*? But in September 2016, while still working on *The Power of the Daleks* Norton said:

---

[302] See Chatterton, Chris, 'Doctor Who: The Ice Warriors' and Rymill, Gavin, 'Evil of the Daleks & Power of the Daleks Scenes'.
[303] 'Lost Doctor Who to return in animated form.'

'We've not got anything lined up after this. We're just focused on getting this done. But obviously the better it performs, the better the case is to then look at doing other **Doctor Who** episodes in future...'[304]

## Context

Even where an old **Doctor Who** story exists in full – such as *The Tomb of the Cybermen*, which followed *The Evil of the Daleks* – we can't quite relive the experience of the original broadcast.

We might try watching the episodes on DVD one at a time, on a weekly basis, rather than all in one go, and in the correct 4:3 aspect ratio. But we're still watching a digital version of the analogue original, with modern sound and picture technology, and probably displayed on a flat screen. TV sets in the 1960s tended to have curved screens, which is why off-air images from *The Evil of the Daleks* show curved rather than angular corners.

Then the context is all wrong. The surviving episode of *The Evil of the Daleks* seems a little old-fashioned and slow in comparison to modern drama. The most obvious difference is that it's in black and white. But the UK's first colour television service was launched on 1 July 1967[305] – five weeks after this episode was first broadcast.

Other sources can help us better understand context. The BBC Genome site has published archive listings for BBC TV and radio programmes. On 27 May 1967, the day episode 2 of *The Evil of the Daleks* was originally broadcast, the celebrities choosing pop hits

---

[304] Norton, interview with author.
[305] See Iain Logie Baird, 'Colour Television in Britain'.

on **Juke Box Jury** were Dusty Springfield, Keith Barron, Judith Chalmers and Mickie Most; there was then a 10-minute news and weather bulletin; then it was **Doctor Who**; then **The Dick Van Dyke Show** and an episode of **The Monkees**. So the Doctor's battles with the Daleks fit into a schedule not of hard-hitting grown-up drama but of light entertainment[306].

But it's not just the context of what else was being broadcast. How we respond to a programme is informed by the world around us, by technology, by culture, by our personal lives and experience, so there's a leap between how we respond to the material today and how the story was received when first broadcast.

But let's put this book in context. It is not, and can't be, a definitive account of *The Evil of the Daleks*. If new sources come to light – photographs, footage, production paperwork, interviews with those involved – they will affect what we understand the story to be, and how we respond to it.

We can't recapture the past, not entirely. And given that it's unlikely the missing episodes of the story will ever be recovered, *The Evil of the Daleks* will always be beyond our grasp. But we can continue to reach.

---

[306] BBC Genome Project.

# ACKNOWLEDGEMENTS

Many people have been extremely generous with their time, memories and archive collections as I wrote this book.

First, thanks to Denise Buckley, Timothy Combe, Frazer Hines, Charlotta Martinus, Chris Thompson, Alexandra Tynan and Anneke Wills for sharing their memories of **Doctor Who** being made 50 years ago.

Thanks also to Samira Ahmed, Mark Ayres, Simon Belcher, Jeremy Bentham, Richard Bignell, Debbie Challis, Sue Cowley, Peter Crocker, Peter Darvill-Evans, Dick Fiddy, Chuck Foster, Rob Francis, Andy Frankham-Allen, Gary Gillatt, James Goss, Peri Godbold, Toby Hadoke, Marcus Hearn, Gary Hopkins, Andy Ledger, Rebecca Levene, Jean-Marc Lofficier, Riona MacNamara, Daniel Milford-Cottam, Jonathan Morris, Patrick Mulkern, Charles Norton, John Peel, Amanda Potter from the Open University, Michael Stevens, Matthew Sweet, Anthony Townsend, Paul Vyse, Stephen James Walker, Jonathan Way, Toby Whithouse, Steven Wickham, John Williams and Paul Winter. Of course, any errors in the text are my responsibility.

Some people also spoke to me off the record. Some directed me to previous interviews or accounts and others, politely, declined to be involved at all. I'm grateful for their time, all the same.

Colin Brockhurst and Gareth Kavanagh let me see material from *Vworp Vworp* in advance of publication. Tom Spilsbury and Peter Ware let me trawl through the archives at DWM. Emma Reeves, Bernie Corbett and Anne Hogben kindly facilitated my search through the cupboards of the Writers' Guild of Great Britain, while

Caroline Barth and Professor Jonathan Powers took me on a tour of Derby Playhouse. I'm extremely grateful for the time and patience of Catherine Gerbrands at *The Stage* and Matthew Chipping and Jeff Walden at BBC Written Archives Centre.

And lastly, thanks to Phil and Stuart at **The Black Archive** for having me, and to Jim Cooray Smith whose book on *The Massacre* made me want to have a go.

# BIBLIOGRAPHY

## Books

Asimov, Isaac, *I, Robot*. 1950. London, Granada Publishing, 1968. ISBN 9780586025321.

Bachman, Maria K, and Don Richard Cox, eds, *Reality's Dark Light: The Sensational Wilkie Collins*. Tennessee, University of Tennessee Press, 2003. ISBN 9781572332744.

> Ceraldi, Gabrielle, 'The Crystal Palace, Imperialism and the "Struggle for Existence": Victorian Evolutionary Discourse in Collins's *The Woman in White*'.

Bentham, Jeremy, *Doctor Who: The Early Years*. London, WH Allen, 1986. ISBN 9780491036122.

The Bible, King James Version. 1611. Oxford, Oxford University Press, 1997. ISBN 9780192835253.

Blackburn, David, and Geoffrey Hollister, eds, *Hutchinson Encyclopedia of Modern Technology*. London, Century Hutchinson Ltd, 1987. ISBN 9780091726072.

Bordwell, David, and Kristin Thompson, *Film Art: An Introduction*. Fifth edition, Boston, McGraw-Hill, 1997. ISBN 9780071140737.

Brend, Mark, *The Sound of Tomorrow: How Electronic Music was Smuggled into the Mainstream*. London, Bloomsbury, 2012. ISBN 9780826424525.

Burgess, Anthony, *A Clockwork Orange*. 1962. London, Penguin Modern Classics, 2013. ISBN 9780141197531.

Carroll, Lewis, ed Martin Gardner, *The Annotated Alice*. London, Random House, 1998. ISBN 9780517189207.

Collins, Wilkie, *The Woman in White*. 1860. Oxford, Oxford University Press, 1980. ISBN 9780192815347.

Collins, Wilkie, *No Name*. 1862. London, Penguin Books Ltd, 1994. ISBN 9780140433975.

Collins, Wilkie, *Heart and Science*. 1883. Stroud, Alan Sutton Publishing Limited, 1994. ISBN 9780862997656.

Conan Doyle, Arthur, *The Penguin Complete Sherlock Holmes*. 1887-1927. London, Penguin Books Ltd, 2009. ISBN 9780141040288.

Condon, Richard, *The Manchurian Candidate*. 1959. London, Orion, 2013. ISBN 9781409147800.

Cooray Smith, James, *The Massacre*. **The Black Archive** #2. Edinburgh, Obverse Books, 2016. ISBN 9781909031388.

Craig, Edward Gordon, *Henry Irving*. London, JM Dent and Sons, 1930.

Dickens, Charles, *Our Mutual Friend*. 1865. London, Penguin Classics 1997. ISBN 9780140434972.

Flick, Vic, *Guitarman: From James Bond to the Beatles and Beyond*. Albany GA, BearManor Media, 2008. ISBN 9781593933081.

Fowles, John, ed Charles Drazin, *John Fowles: The Journals Volume 2*. Evanston IL, Northwestern University Press, 2009. ISBN 9780810125155.

Hearn, Marcus, *Doctor Who: The Vault*. London, BBC Books, 2013. ISBN 9781849905817.

Hulke, Malcolm and Terrance Dicks, *The Making of Doctor Who*. London, W H Allen, 1972. ISBN 9780426116158.

Kukula, Marek, and Simon Guerrier, *The Scientific Secrets of Doctor Who*. London, BBC Books, 2015. ISBN 9781849909389.

Lofficer, Jean-Marc, *The Doctor Who Programme Guide Volume 1*. London, WH Allen, 1981. ISBN 9780491028042.

MacDonald, Ian, *Revolution in the Head: The Beatles' Records and the Sixties*. 1994. London, Vintage, 2008. ISBN 9780099526797.

Marcus, Steven, *The Other Victorians: A Study of Sexuality and Pornography in Mid-Nineteenth-Century England*. London, Weidenfeld and Nicolson, 1966.

Mayer, David, ed, *Henry Irving and The Bells: Irving's Personal Script of the Play*. Manchester, Manchester University Press, 1980. ISBN 0719007984.

Goring, Marius, 'Foreword'.

Meadows, Jack, *The Victorian Scientist: The Growth of a Profession*. London, the British Library, 2004. ISBN 0712308946.

Molesworth, Richard, *Wiped! Doctor Who's Missing Episodes*. 2010. Second edition, Prestatyn, Telos Publishing Ltd, February 2013. ISBN 9781845830809.

Nation, Terry, and David Whitaker, *The Dalek Book*. London, Souvenir Press, 1964. No ISBN.

Nation, Terry, and Brad Ashton, *The Dalek Outer Space Book*. London, Souvenir Press, 1966. No ISBN.

Peel, John, *Doctor Who: The Evil of the Daleks*. **The Target Doctor Who Library** #155. London, Target Books, 1993. ISBN 9780426203896.

Pixley, Andrew, *The Saint: Original Soundtrack Notes*. Lea Valley, Network Distributing, 2010. No ISBN.

Rayner, Jacqueline, ed, *Doctor Who: Short Trips – Farewells*. Maidenhead, Big Finish, 2006. ISBN 978-1844351510.

> Lyons, Steve, 'Father Figure'.

Rees, Dylan, *Downtime: The Lost Years of Doctor Who*. Edinburgh, Obverse Books, 2017. ISBN 9781909031425.

Richardson, Michael, *The Champions: Programme Notes*. Lea Valley, Network Distribution, 2006. No ISBN.

Richardson, Michael, *Department S: Programme Notes*. Lea Valley, Network Distribution, 2008. No ISBN.

Richardson, Michael, *Bowler Hats and Kinky Boots: The Unofficial and Unauthorised Guide to the Avengers*. Prestatyn, Telos, 2014. ISBN 9781845830977.

Sandbrook, Dominic, *White Heat: A History of Britain in the Swinging Sixties*. 2006. London, Abacus, 2007. ISBN 9780349118208.

Sweet, Matthew, *Inventing the Victorians*. London, Faber & Faber, 2002. ISBN 9780571206636.

Tribe, Steve, and James Goss, *Doctor Who: The Dalek Handbook*. London, BBC Books, 2011. ISBN 9781849902328.

Truffaut, François, *Hitchcock/Truffaut: A Definitive Study of Alfred Hitchcock*. New York, Simon & Schuster, 1986. ISBN 9780671604295.

Turner, Alwyn, *Terry Nation: The Man Who Invented the Daleks*. London, Aurum Press, 2013. ISBN 9781781310410.

Watling, Deborah, with Paul WT Ballard, *Daddy's Girl: The Autobiography*. Coventry, Fantom Films, 2010. ISBN 9781906263416.

Whitaker, David, *Doctor Who in an Exciting Adventure with the Daleks*. 1964. *Doctor Who and the Daleks*. **The Target Doctor Who Library** #16. London, Target, 1973. ISBN 9780426101109.

Wills, Anneke, *Self Portrait: My Journey As An Actress, Wife And Mother In The Swinging Sixties*. Andover, Hirst Books, September 2007. ISBN 9780955714900.

Wilson, AN, *The Victorians*. 2002. London, Arrow Books, 2003. ISBN 9780099451860.

Woolley, Benjamin, *Ada Lovelace: Bride of Science – Romance, Reason and Byron's Daughter*. 1999. London, Pan, 2015. ISBN 9781447272540.

Yapp, Nick, *The Write Stuff: A History of the Writers Guild of Great Britain 1959-2009*. London, The Writers' Guild of Great Britain, 2009. ISBN 9781906192372.

## Periodicals

*Doctor Who Magazine* (DWM). Marvel UK, Panini, BBC, 1979-.

Cover. DWM #367, cover date March 2006.

*The Dalek Chronicles*, DWM Summer Special, cover date August 1994.

'Innes Lloyd'. DWM Winter Special, 1983.

Auger, David, and Stephen James Walker, 'Back to Basics'. DWM #141, cover date October 1988.

Barnes, Alan, 'The Fact of Fiction: Lead into Gold – The Evil of the Daleks'. DWM #342, cover date April 2004.

Bentley, Chris, 'Your Own Dalek'. *Doctor Who 50 Years* #1: *The Daleks*, cover date May 2013.

Cook, Benjamin, 'The DWM Interview: Great Scot'. DWM #458, cover date April 2013.

Gray, Scott, *Children of the Revolution*. DWM #312 to #317, cover date January to May 2002.

Gray, Warwick, 'Bringer of Darkness'. DWM Summer Special 1993.

Guerrier, Simon, 'Secret Armies'. *The Essential Doctor Who* #9: *Invasions Of Earth*, cover date October 2016.

Hearn, Marcus, 'What The Papers Said'. DWM #200, cover date June 1993.

Hearn, Marcus, 'Alchemy and Apocalypse'. *Doctor Who Magazine* #265, cover date June 1998.

Hopkins, Gary, 'A Personal Note'. DWM #200, cover date June 1993.

Kibble-White, Graham, 'The DWM Review: Missing in Action – The Evil of the Daleks'. DWM #498, cover date May 2016.

Marson, Richard, 'Deborah Watling Interview: Archetypal Heroine'. DWM #87, cover date April 1984.

Marson, Richard, 'Whitaker's World of Doctor Who'. DWM #98, cover date March 1985.

Marson, Richard, 'Martinus & Maloney'. DWM #108, cover date January 1986.

Marson, Richard, 'Gerry Davis Interviewed'. DWM #124, cover date May 1997.

Morris, Jonathan and Pereira, Matthew, 'The Telesnap Archive: The Evil of the Daleks'. DWM Special edition #36 *The Missing Episodes: The Second Doctor Volume 2*, cover date December 2013.

Mulkern, Patrick, 'Nostalgia: The Evil of the Daleks'. DWM #128, cover date September 1987.

Mulkern, Patrick and Richard Marson, 'King of the Tracks', DWM Winter Special (1985)

Nazarro, Joe, 'Interview: Terry Nation'. DWM #145, cover date February 1989.

Pixley, Andrew, 'Doctor Who Archive Feature: Serial LL, *The Evil of the Daleks*'. DWM #200, cover date June 1993.

Pixley, Andrew, 'Archive Extra'. DWM Special Edition #4: *The Complete Second Doctor*, cover date June 2003.

Pixley, Andrew, 'Daleks: Invasion USA 1967AD', DWM #406, cover date April 2009.

Rigelsford, Adrian, 'Interview: Tim Combe'. DWM 10th Anniversary Special, cover date October 1989.

Rigelsford, Adrian, 'Producing Who: Innes Lloyd'. DWM #180, cover date October 1991.

Townsend, Anthony, 'Acting the Part: Pauline Collins'. DWM #212, cover date May 1994.

Troughton, Michael, 'Michael Troughton's Memories: Part One – Top of the Pops', DWM #306, cover date July 2001.

Walker, Jane, 'Leatherlungs is Back'. DWM #212, cover date May 1994.

*Nothing at the End of the Lane.*

Bignell, Richard, 'The Evil of the Daleks'. *Nothing at the End of the Lane* #3, January 2012.

Pixley, Andrew, 'Trouble in Store'. *Nothing at the End of the Lane* #4, Autumn 2015.

*The Stage and Television Today (The Stage).*

Television Today. #431, 25 May 1967.

Caption to a photograph of Marius Goring. *The Stage*, 4 May 1967.

'Jo, the Girl who "Dared", plays Liza'. *The Stage*, 22 April 1965.

Bilbow, Marjorie, 'Dr. Who and a Succession of Delightful Monsters'. *The Stage*, 18 May 1967.

Edmund, Bill, 'Liza as a Good, Lusty Fast-Moving Musical'. *The Stage*, 29 April 1965.


*The Times*.

'Court Circular'. *The Times*, 23 May 1967.

'The Daleks Come To Life'. *The Times*, 22 December 1965.

'Personal', *The Times*, 26 May 1967.

'Whose Theatre Is it?'. *The Times*, 29 April 1967.

Billington, Michael, 'Repertory Alive and Kicking'. *The Times*, 6 May 1967.

Wardle, Irving, 'Lewis's Spine-Chiller Retains its Force'. *The Times*, 26 April 1967.

*Radio Times*. BBC Magazines, Immediate Media Company 1921-.

*Doctor Who 10th Anniversary Special*, November 1973.

*Vworp Vworp*.

Ashton, Brad, 'A Cheque on the Table', *Vworp Vworp* #3, March 2017.

Brockhurst, Colin, 'The Ideas Boy', *Vworp Vworp* #3, March 2017.

Scoones, Paul, 'Telesnapped!', *Vworp Vworp* #3, March 2017.

'The Coming Quarter: What Some Guild Members Will Be Working On In The Next Three Months'. *Guild News: The Journal of the Television & Screen Writers' Guild*, 5 June 1961.

'Extraordinary General Meeting: The ITV Royalties Battle; Two New Branches; A New Name, & New Rules'. *Screenwriter* 18 Autumn 1965.

'June Wedding for David Whitaker'. *The Screenwriter Quarterly* #11, Winter 1962-63.

'Someone's Stolen the TARDIS!!'. *DWB: The Journal of British Telefantasy* #94, October 1991.

Anderson, Carl David, 'The Positive Electron'. *Physical Review* #43, 15 March 1933.

Howe-Wallace, Philip, 'Summoned by Bells'. *The Guardian*, 27 April 1967.

Pixley, Andrew, 'The Invaders'. *The Essential Doctor Who* #9: *Invasions of Earth* October 2016.

Shorter, Eric, 'Spine-Chiller of 1871 Still Good Today'. *The Telegraph*, 28 April 1967.

Whitaker, David, uncredited, **The Daleks**. *TV Century 21*, 1965-67.

## Television

**Adam Adamant Lives!** BBC, 1966-67.

**The Avengers**. Associated British Corporation, 1961-69.

**The Baron**. ITC, 1965-7.

**Class**. BBC, 2016-.

    *For Tonight We Might Die*, 2016.

**Doctor Who**. BBC, 1963-.

    *The Daleks*, 1963-64.

'Creation of the Daleks'. Extra on the 2006 DVD release.

*The Chase*, 1965.

'Daleks Beyond the Screen'. Extra on the 2010 DVD release.

*The Tenth Planet*, 1966.

DVD commentary.

*The Faceless Ones*, 1967.

*The War Games*, 1969.

'The Doctor's Composer'. Extra on the 2009 DVD release.

*Terror of the Autons*, 1971.

'Life on Earth'. Extra on the 2011 DVD release.

*Daleks – The Early Years*. BBC Video release 1992.

*Lost in Time*. DVD box set, 2004.

**The Forsyte Saga**. BBC, 1967.

**Monty Python's Flying Circus**. BBC, 1969-74.

*Live from the Grill-o-Mat*, 1970.

*Resistance is Useless*. BBC, 1992.

**Sir Arthur Conan Doyle**. BBC, 1967.

*The Beetle Hunter*, 1967.

**The Saint**. ITC, 1962-9.

**The Wednesday Play**. BBC, 1964-70.

*Alice*, 1965.

## Film

Flemyng, Gordon, dir, *Dr Who and the Daleks*. AARU Productions, Amicus Productions, 1965.

Flemyng, Gordon, *Daleks: Invasion Earth 2150AD*. AARU Productions, British Lion Films, Amicus Productions, 1966.

Frankenheimer, John, dir, *The Manchurian Candidate*. United Artists, 1962.

Gilbert, Lewis, dir, *You Only Live Twice.* Eon Productions, 1967.

Hamilton, Guy, dir, *Goldfinger*. Eon Productions, 1964.

Neill, Roy William, dir, *Sherlock Holmes in Washington*. Universal Pictures, 1943.

Reeves, Michael, dir, *The Sorcerers*. Curtwel Productions, Global, Tigon, 1967.

## Stage Plays

Lewis, Leopold, *The Bells*. 1871.

Whitaker, David, *The Curse of the Daleks*, 1965.

## Audio CD and Cassette

*Doctor Who: The Missing Stories – The Evil of the Daleks*. BBC Audio Collection 1992.

*Doctor Who: The Lost Stories – The Second Doctor Box Set*. Big Finish Productions, December 2010.

*Doctor Who: The Lost TV Episodes — Collection Four*. Audio GO, 2 February 2012.

## Music

The Beatles, *Sgt. Pepper's Lonely Heart Club Band*. Parlophone, 1967.

## Radio

*My Life as a Dalek*, BBC Radio 4, 29 July 2003.

## Web

'Alfred Hitchcock: The Difference Between Mystery and Suspense'. American Film Institute channel, YouTube, 5 August 2009. https://www.youtube.com/watch?v=-Xs111uH9ss. Accessed 4 November 2016.

'Andrew's Collection'. AndrewLloydWebber.com. http://www.andrewlloydwebber.com/art/andrews-collection/. Accessed 4 November 2016.

BBC Genome Project. http://genome.ch.bbc.co.uk/. Accessed 23 July 2016.

'Sir Arthur Conan Doyle: The Beetle Hunter'. http://genome.ch.bbc.co.uk/2fbda8f6dba9430e96875afc7a0d6d9d. Accessed 4 November 2016.

Listings for BBC One on Saturday 27 May 1967. http://genome.ch.bbc.co.uk/schedules/bbcone/london/1967-05-27. Accessed 4 November 2016.

'Beryl Vertue'. Hartswood Films.
http://www.hartswoodfilms.co.uk/about-us/beryl-vertue/.
Accessed 4 November 2016.

'Doctor Who Director Derek Martinus Dies Aged 82'. BBC News, 28
March 2014. http://www.bbc.co.uk/news/entertainment-arts-
26789825. Accessed 4 November 2016.

'Doctor Who Photonovels: The Evil of the Daleks'.
http://www.bbc.co.uk/doctorwho/classic/photonovels/evilofthedal
eks/. Accessed 4 November 2016.

'The Doctor Who Transcripts'.
http://www.chakoteya.net/DoctorWho/index.html. Accessed 4
November 2016.

'The Evil of the Daleks'. BBC **Doctor Who** website.
http://www.bbc.co.uk/programmes/p00krdg6. Accessed 7
November 2016.

'The Evil of the Daleks Film Trim'.
https://www.youtube.com/watch?v=dEHb_jp4uB8. Accessed 4
November 2016.

'The Evil of the Daleks Stage Show'.
http://www.evilofthedaleks.co.uk/the-evil-of-the-daleks-stage-
show.html. Accessed 4 November 2016.

'FILM: It Happened Here'. Reel Streets.
http://www.reelstreets.com/index.php/component/films/?task=vi
ew&id=487&film_ref=it_happened_here&start=60. Accessed 4
November 2016.

'"Hearing" to "Helmond"', The Project Gutenberg EBook of Encyclopaedia Britannica, 11th Edition, Volume 13, Slice 2. http://gutenberg.readingroo.ms/3/9/5/2/39521/39521-h/39521-h.htm. Accessed 4 November 2016.

'Heritage'. Laura Ashley. http://www.lauraashley.com/uk/about-laura-ashley/heritage/page/heritage. Accessed 4 November 2016.

'History'. Grim's Dyke Hotel. http://www.grimsdyke.com/about-us/history/. Accessed 4 November 2016.

'Houses with Artistic Connections'. *Country Life*, 31 May 2007. http://www.countrylife.co.uk/property/guides-advice/houses-with-artistic-connections-39935. Accessed 4 November 2016.

'Interview with Isaac Asimov.' Public Resource Org channel, YouTube, 25 December 2009. https://www.youtube.com/watch?v=4gn3MyTE80A. Accessed 4 November 2016.

'An interview with John Peel.' Recorded for the Loose Cannon reconstruction of *The Evil of the Daleks* in 2008. http://www.dailymotion.com/video/x3o5tlb. Accessed 22 November 2016.

'The London Gazette, 1st July 1969.' The Gazette: Official Public Record. https://www.thegazette.co.uk/London/issue/44886/page/6802/data.pdf. Accessed 7 November 2016.

'Lost Doctor Who to return in animated form.' BBC News, 7 September 2016. http://www.bbc.co.uk/news/entertainment-arts-37285820. Accessed 4 November 2016.

'John Barry'. In Tune Sound of Cinema, BBC Radio 3. 16 September 2013. http://www.bbc.co.uk/programmes/p02r6j90. Accessed 4 November 2016.

'The New Dr Who.' BBC Archive. http://www.bbc.co.uk/archive/changingwho/10305.shtml. Accessed 4 November 2016.

'Photos YOLT recording (2)'. John Barry: The Man With the Midas Touch. 10 April 2015. http://www.johnbarry.org.uk/index.php/photos/you-only-live-twice-full-size-recording-session-photo/itemlist/category/55-photos-yolt-recording. Accessed 4 November 2016.

'Brainwash Culture'. Sunday Feature, BBC Radio 3. 13 March 2016. http://www.bbc.co.uk/programmes/b0739rh0. Accessed 7 November 2016.

'What is Missing?' http://missingepisodes.blogspot.co.uk/p/what-is-missing.html. Accessed 4 November 2016.

Baird, Iain Logie, 'Colour Television in Britain'. National Media Museum, May 2011. http://www.nationalmediamuseum.org.uk/~/media/Files/NMeM/PDF/Collections/Television/ColourTelevisionInBritain.pdf. Accessed 4 November 2016.

Bordwell, David, 'Hitchcock, Lessing and the Bomb Under the Table'. David Bordwell's Website on Cinema, 29 November 2013. http://www.davidbordwell.net/blog/2013/11/29/hitchcock-lessing-and-the-bomb-under-the-table/. Accessed 4 November 2016.

Chatterton, Chris, 'Doctor Who: The Ice Warriors'. www.chrischatterton.com/doctor-who/. Accessed 4 November 2016.

Dickens, Charles, 'The Noble Savage'. Dickens Journal Online. http://www.djo.org.uk/household-words/volume-vii/page-337.html. Accessed 4 November 2016.

Foster, Chuck, 'Grim's Dyke Hotel'. http://www.doctorwholocations.net/locations/grimsdykehotel. Accessed 4 November 2016.

Gillatt, Gary, 'The Underwater Menace episode 3 & Galaxy 4: Airlock'. Squabbling Rubber. https://gillatt.wordpress.com/2012/02/28/the-underwater-menace-episode-2-galaxy-4-airlock/. Accessed 4 November 2016.

Green, Jon, and Gav Rymill, 'Evil of the Daleks: Events from Apr 67 to Jul 67'. http://www.dalek6388.co.uk/evil-of-the-daleks/. Accessed 4 November 2016.

Gonzalez, Susan, 'Director Spike Lee Slams "Same Old" Black Stereotypes in Today's Films'. *Yale Bulletin & Callendar*, 2 March 2001. https://web.archive.org/web/20090121190429/http://www.yale.edu/opa/arc-ybc/v29.n21/story3.html. Accessed 4 November 2016.

Guerrier, Simon, 'Off Air Images from *The Evil of the Daleks*'. http://obversebooks.co.uk/theblackarchive/available-titles/11-evil/off-air-images-from-the-evil-of-the-daleks/. Accessed 6 March 2017.

Hattenstone, Simon, 'Pauline Collins: From Shirley Valentine to Dustin Hoffman'. *The Guardian* 11 December 2012.

https://www.theguardian.com/film/2012/dec/11/pauline-collins-quartet-interview. Accessed 4 November 2016.

Hines, Frazer. Tweet posted 12:10pm, 15 April 2013. https://twitter.com/WhoFrazer/status/323755130048630784. Accessed 4 November 2016.

Howe, David, 'Doctor Who Toybox'. http://www.doctorwhotoybox.co.uk/. Accessed 4 November 2016.

Kukula, Marek, and Simon Guerrier, 'The Science of Doctor Who: What Do Daleks Smell Like?'. Sci-Fi Now, 29 May 2015. https://www.scifinow.co.uk/books/simon-guerrier-dr-marek-kukula-on-what-daleks-smell-like/. Accessed 4 November 2016.

Langford, David, 'Dangerous Thoughts'. Originally published in Foundation #4, 1990. Ansible. http://ansible.uk/writing/positron.html. Accessed 4 November 2016.

Moffat, Steven, 'Steven Moffat on *The Evil of the Daleks*'. **Doctor Who** Advent(ure) Calendar 2012, BBC **Doctor Who** website, 4 December 2012. http://www.bbc.co.uk/programmes/p01240sf. Accessed 4 November 2016.

Mulkern, Patrick, 'Doctor Who story guide – The Evil of the Daleks'. *Radio Times*. http://www.radiotimes.com/blog/2009-06-14/the-evil-of-the-daleks. Accessed 4 November 2016.

Nicholls, Peter, and David Langford, 'Positronic robots'. *The Encyclopedia of Science Fiction*. http://www.sf-encyclopedia.com/entry/positronic_robots. Accessed 4 November 2016.

Norris, Alastair, 'JHP Ltd v BBC Worldwide Ltd, Trustees of the Estate of Terry Nation'. England and Wales High Court (Chancery Division) Decisions, 16 April 2008. http://alpha.bailii.org/ew/cases/EWHC/Ch/2008/757.html. Accessed 4 November 2016.

Pearson, Hugh M, *Doctor Who Reconstructions: The Lost Lords of Time – Recons, Volume One (2014)*. http://homepages.bw.edu/~jcurtis/TLLOT-Recons-VolumeOne-June2014.pdf. Accessed 4 November 2016.

Preddle, John, and John Lavalie, eds, 'New Zealand'. *BroaDWcast*. http://gallifreybase.com/w/index.php/New_Zealand Accessed 4 November 2016.

Roberts, Steve, 'Lost in Time – DVD Boxset'. Restoration Team website, 10 October 2004. http://restorationteam.impossiblethings.net/lostintime.htm. Accessed 4 November 2016.

Rudin, Dave, 'Archive Interview with Terry Nation!' Kasterborous, 2 February 2014. http://kasterborous.com/2014/02/archive-interview-terry-nation/. Accessed 4 November 2016.

Rymill, Gavin, 'Evil of the Daleks & Power of the Daleks Scenes'. The Mind Robber: Missing Episodes Reconstructions. www.themindrobber.co.uk/power-of-the-daleks-missing-episodes-reconstruction.html. Accessed 4 November 2016.

Scoones, Paul, 'The making of... *More than 30 Years in the TARDIS*'. http://doctorwho.org.nz/archive/tsv43/30yearsinthetardis.html. Accessed 4 November 2016.

Stevens, Alan, 'Donald Tosh Interview'. Kaldor City. www.kaldorcity.com/people/dtinterview.html. Accessed 25 March 2016.

Vincent-Rudzki, Jan, and Stephen Payne, 'Interview: Gerry Davis'. DWAS Online. http://www.dwasonline.co.uk/node/442?cat=voices_from_the_pa st. Accessed 4 November 2016.

Williams, Ian, 'Frequently Asked Questions (FAQ) Page'. Restoration Team website. http://www.iwillvoice.com/faqpage.html. Accessed 4 November 2016.

Wilson, Donald, 'Concept Notes for New SF Drama'. BBC Archive: The Genesis of **Doctor Who**. http://www.bbc.co.uk/archive/doctorwho/6402.shtml?page=1. Accessed 4 November 2016.

# BIOGRAPHY

Simon Guerrier is the co-author of *Whographica* and *The Scientific Secrets of Doctor Who* for BBC Books. When not writing **Doctor Who** books, audio plays and whatever else, he makes documentaries for Radio 3.